Time to Grow up and Act Like A Man

Steps every teenage boy can take now to ensure a successful and smooth transition into Manhood

Andrew K. Coakley

DEDICATION

This book is dedicated to two of the greatest blessings in my life – my two sons Tayvon and Traedyn. They have been the rainbow during my cloudy and rainy days.
And to my wife Monique, who has been the pot of gold at the end of that rainbow. She has been my biggest fan and supporter in the writing of this book. And she has been patient and loving in my transition into manhood.
To all the teenage boys who are on the brink of making one of the toughest transition in their lives. It can be a smooth transition once you know what to expect and once you have the knowledge that will prepare you for Manhood. Become the man you were created to be.

Table of Contents

You're not Peter Pan

Rites of Passage – when does a boy become a man?

Warning, choose your friends carefully

Choosing the right career path

The Golden Rule

Searching for love – dealing with the dating scene

Do not awaken love before its time

Becoming a man of your word

A little respect goes a long way

Everyone pays a price for the decisions that they make

Don't be afraid to dream and dream big

Live your life in balance

Be skillful with your hands

Here is the bottom line

Unless You're Peter Pan, Someday You Will Be Required To Grow Up

You are not Peter Pan.
Peter Pan is the fictional, cartoon character whose deepest desire was to never, ever grow up. Peter Pan wanted to remain a boy for as long as he lived and in the world of make believe, he was able to do just that.
But you don't live in a world of make believe and no, you're not Peter Pan.
In other words, all things being equal, you are going to one day leave boyhood and enter manhood, whether you want to or not. The question is, are you ready for that?
You're thinking, "what's the big deal, I will eventually go from the stage of being a boy to being a man". Wait a minute, that's not necessarily true and such a transition is way more complicated than people make it out to be.
When I became a teenager, as a boy, I, along with the generation of boys whom I grew up with, were all bombarded with statements that confused us. We were always hearing phrases like; "why don't you act like men?", "grow up and be men" or "you're getting older now, you need to be more responsible and act like men".
Although we never really understood what those comments meant, we tried our best to "act like men". It wasn't until I reached my early 30s that I realized that back then we were asked to be something we had never seen.
You see, the majority of the boys in our neighborhoods grew up without our fathers present in our homes. We were raised by single moms who did their best to keep us on the right path, and while they did their best to raise us right, they could not teach us how to be men.
When you live in a home where there is no man present, you have very little concept of what a man's role really is. When you live in a society where many of its men have abandoned their responsibilities, you have very little idea of what a man's role is within a community or in society.
So, as boys we grew up being asked to be something we had never seen. We did not know how to be men, but it was assumed that once we reached a certain age, we would automatically become men. Boy, were we wrong…dead wrong.
Do you find yourself in that situation, where you're expected to "be a man", but you have no idea what that means? Then, this book has been written specifically for you, because its purpose is to teach you how to cross that dimension from boyhood to manhood.
It will teach you some of the things you need to do now to prepare you for when that time comes for you to "grow up and become a man."
There are certain steps you can take now that will put you in a better position to take on the responsibility as a man. You can become the kind of man whom everyone respects and who other young boys can look up too and emulate.
But manhood is not automatic.
The physical structural growth of a boy to an "adult male" may be automatic, but becoming a man is not. Just look around and it's easy to see how true that is. For years, centuries even, it's been assumed that boys automatically become men. There was the assumption that if you leave a boy alone he will eventually grow into a man.

However, the amount of broken, confused, defeated and childish males in our society proves that the transition from boyhood to manhood is not something that automatically happens. It has to be a planned, or organized transition.

It's easy to point to a successful businessman, who came from a poor family, was raised on his own, went on to establish a number of businesses and accumulate so much wealth and say there is a self-made man.

But while that man has mastered the art of business life and has indeed become wealthy, no one may see the character flaws that make him a terrible father, an unfaithful husband, or a bad friend. He has mastered one part of manhood, but has fallen short in so many other areas.

The truth is manhood is something that is learned. Boys must be taught how to become men. Why? Because there are so many aspects to manhood that just leaving a boy to himself and hoping he becomes a "good" man in the future is like shooting in the dark.

The statistics of the amount of boys and men who end up in prisons around the world proves that the male species is lacking something and somewhere along the line they are falling through the cracks. If manhood was automatic, the prisons would not consume so many of our males.

Manhood is tough, but remaining a boy in a man's body in a tough, unforgiving world is even harder.

But the truth is manhood is only tough for those who have not prepared for it.

Let me begin by being frank and up front with you; life is tough. There are a lot of rules to follow and apply if you hope to succeed in this maze called life. However, once you know the rules, and learn to apply them, then life is not all that hard. It is when you are playing a game where you don't know or understand the rules, which can cause you to become confused, discouraged, broken and defeated.

This is the reason why I wanted to write you these words, to fill you in on some of the rules, or steps you can take to help you become the kind of man many only dream of being.

Don't take these steps lightly because this kind of information is something many men today wish they knew when they were just boys. I failed to learn this information in my younger years and because of this lack of information, I, like so many other men, suffered greatly.

I grew up as a confused boy into a defeated man. No one taught me about life. There was no one there to guide me through the maze of making the right decisions, choosing the right career, the right mate or even the right kind of car.

Yes, believe it or not, all of these may sound like simple decisions, but once you begin to live life, you will find that making the wrong choices, even in the simplest of things, can lead to a life of misery and pain; a life of regret and a feeling of being trapped.

I had to learn the hard way.

There are so many men sitting in a jail cell somewhere wishing they had someone in their life to show them the right way. They wished that they had someone there to help them make the right choices in life. They wished that they had access to the kind of information that you will receive in this book.

No, I don't claim to know it all. Even now, as I get older, there is still a lot I don't know or understand and that is because life is constantly changing every day, there is so much to learn each day. But even with the many changes in culture, era and environment, there are some rules to life that never change.

Certain rules are universal; they mean the same where ever you may go. It's like the truth of multiplication – no matter where in the world you go, two times two will always be four.

Consider this book to be like a reference material, to which you can always look up some kind of advice for something that you may be facing at that point in time.

You see, every stage of life has its ups and downs and how you come out of one stage will determine how you think, how you grow and advance into the next stage. And yes, each stage of life is important.

However, if you are like me, chances are you may not have a father around (for whatever reason) to give you the kind of advice that you will need. If you are fortunate enough to have your dad around and he is there to give you sound advice, then consider yourself Blessed and learn to appreciate your dad.

But if you have no positive male influence around to guide you, then consider this book as words of wisdom from someone who has been around long enough to learn from my mistakes, the same mistakes you can avoid.

So many decisions await you ahead and how you decide will determine your outcome in life. It is my prayer that not only will you use this information to prepare for manhood, but that you would discover your purpose early in your life and pursue it with passion, courage and wisdom.

I pray that you would grow into a teen with a mind of his own, who never gives in to peer pressure and that you would eventually grow into a productive, strong, well-mannered, well-respected young man, who someday will become the man whom God intended for you to be. If you listen to these instructions and follow them, then perhaps you can come through these tough teenage years unscathed and prepared to take on the task of manhood.

Okay, now that we've gotten that out of the way, are you ready to make some changes in your life that will help you to be prepared for the next stage of your life? Believe me, once you put in place the foundation you will need in the future, life will become so sweet for you, there may be a few people who will envy you for living life so good.

Here we go.

The Rite of Passage – When Does A Boy Become A Man?

It is the kind of coming of age ceremony that would crawl your flesh and make you think twice about what it means to become a man.

In the Manda Okipa tribe, a Mandan boy would fast for about four days in a hut all by himself in preparation for the Rites of Passage ceremony that would be witnessed by all of the members of the tribe.

The elders of the tribe would take the young boy and pierce his chest, shoulder, and back muscles with large wooden splints. To these splints ropes, which are attached to the roof of the hut, are attached to the splints and in what can only be considered something from a horror flick, the boy is raised in the air as the ropes are pulled through the roof and through the splints attached to his body.

There he would hang, suspended in midair by the ropes and the splints, which would begin to pull through his flesh. One can only imagine the kind of pain that passes though the boy's body as it is suspended in midair.

Through all of this, one of the requirements in order for the boy to pass the test is that he must not grimace in pain, because if he does, he would not be considered having passed the test of manhood.

While the boy is suspended into the air, elders of the tribe would hammer more splints through his arms and legs. The boy would grit his teeth in pain, but would do his best not to cry out in pain. As a result, the boy would faint from the pain.

Once he becomes unconscious, the boy would be lowered down from the roof of the hut and the ropes are removed.

It gets worse.

Once the boy regains consciousness, the elders would take his pinky finger and chop it off in one swift movement. The finger is believed to be a sacrificial gift to the gods.

The coming of age ceremony would end with the boy, who had endured all of that pain, running around in a circle, which was formed by the villagers. As he ran, the villagers would reach out and grab the embedded splints that were still in the boy's body, ripping them out, causing even more pain.

In spite of what some would consider to be an act of torture and in spite of all the pain he had to endure, the boy, even in a weak state, would consider the event one of the greatest in his life, because then he was considered to be a man.

Imagine having to endure this kind of ritual before you are considered to be a man.

Yet, these types of Coming of Age rituals are common among tribes and cultures in certain parts of the world. Just about all of the rituals involve some very painful activities.

For instance, for the Vanuatu people there is a ritual called land jumping. It's similar to bungee jumping, except that instead of rubber chords they use tree vines and the objective is to come as close to death as possible. The jumper's goal is to brush his head on the ground; if he survives, he's considered to be a man.

Here are some more examples of such coming of age rituals:
- Men of the Hamar tribe in Ethiopa before they are allowed to marry, they have to go through a strange ritual. First, the young boy's closest female friends and family chant while they are whipped by the men of the tribe. The scars that are left on their backs are meant to be a testament to the pain they were willing to endure for the initiate. Afterwards, four castrated bulls are lined side by side, the naked boy runs across their backs, and voila…he's a man.

- Many aboriginal tribes of Australia send their young men into the wilderness for up to six months to test whether they are ready to become men. The boys must survive, unassisted, and keep themselves totally isolated. When they return after six months they will be considered men of the tribe.

- As soon as the time comes for boys of the Matis tribe in Brazil to go on the hunt they have a bitter poison dumped in their eyes in order to "improve" their vision. After this they are beaten and whipped. Finally they must endure the excruciating conclusion to the trial in which they inject themselves with the poison of the Giant Leaf Frog using wooden needles.

- Young Fula boys must undergo a whipping battle in which they trade blows with another boy from a different tribe in order to become a man. The sticks they use to whip each other have sharpened points and thorns all over them to maximize the pain they inflict, and both boys attempt to take the blows without wincing or showing any signs of weakness. The boy whom the observing crowd deems the winner is considered the bravest, and earns the right to be called a man.

- Scarification is something practiced by the Sepik River tribes in Papua New Guinea as part of an initiation ceremony for men. This is only a small part of a ceremony that lasts weeks and includes public humiliation, but it's ridiculously painful. The elders of the tribe use razor blades to cut the young men all over their bodies in a pattern that closely imitates the rough skin of an alligator. They believe that the alligator will then consume any semblance of a boy left in their bodies, and they will become men.

- When it is time for a young Mardudjara aborigine to enter manhood, he is led by the tribe's elders to a secluded place. While one of the elders sits on his chest another will slice off the boy's foreskin. After enduring this without any form of anesthesia, the boy is then given his foreskin, and must swallow it without chewing. After the circumcision heals the boy is led to an isolated area again where the underside of his penis is cut down to the scrotum and he must stand, bleeding, over a fire. Welcome to manhood.

Here in the Western world, such rituals are considered to be barbaric, and rightly so, however, the bottom line of each ritual is an attempt by the leaders or the elders to pinpoint a point in a boy's life when he is considered to become a man.
Closer to home, the ritual of circumcision is still a common practice, but because the activity is done to a boy when he is still a baby, it is not done to represent manhood. It is more of a religious activity than anything else.
So, how do we here in the Western World determine when a boy becomes a man?

There is the "Sweet 16" parties, and far from torture, these events could include drinking of alcoholic beverages, along with the giving of sometimes expensive gifts. This is the way we say a teenager has crossed over the threshold into manhood.

What other ways do we consider to be Rites of Passage or a transition from boyhood to manhood? Some say it happens when you graduate from high school, when you grow a beard of a moustache, when you get a driver's license, when you get a car, when you get a job, when you have a child or when you lose your virginity.

There used to be a question of "at what age does a boy become a man"? Some say at the age of eight, some say at the age of 13, and some say at the age of 18.

But look at the way many of these boys who reach these ages behave, and there is no denying that the actions of these boys, in many cases remains childish. Of course, it would be insane to consider an eight year old to have reached the level of manhood.

A 13-year-old is still considered a child and although the popular age of 16 or 18 is considered to be the middle ground, the truth is many teens at this age still make questionable decisions.

On the other hand, there are many "men" in their 30s and 40s who still act like children. Many of them make childish decisions and only think of the now, never planning for the future.

There are grown "men" who have problems with discipline and who cannot hold down a job. They may be grown physically, but mentally, they are still thinking like children.

There are grown-ups still living with their parents, sometimes may not be for the reason of being there to assist their parents, but really they are living there because they have failed to grow up and take on responsibilities of adults.

I believe that just like many of the barbaric actions of many tribes and cultures around the world still does not make one a man, age really does not determine that either.

To me, becoming a man is more than just one's age, but rather manhood involves adopting a certain mindset, the way one responds to responsibilities and the way one reacts to the circumstances of life.

While these actions or the age numbers may be used as a marker, no one really knows exactly when a boy crosses over to manhood.

The torture type activities of the Manda Okipa tribe does not guarantee a boy moves into manhood. A boy from the tribe can go through all of that pain and when he is faced with a tough decision, could still make a choice out of his childish mind, which, by the way does not change even after the Rites of Passage ceremony.

A 12-year-old boy does not go asleep on the eve of his birthday and awakens at 13 suddenly as a man. He too, once faced with a tough decision, will still think as a 12 year-old.

Even the laws of the land proves that children of certain age are not at a point where they are able to make adult decisions. One has to be 16 to get a driver's license and the age of sexual consent is 17. Ironically, to participate in these activities before the time frame is considered against the law.

I used to watch a television show about teenage girls who become pregnant and the show told their stories and how they dealt with all of the issues that accompany motherhood. One thing I have noticed in these shows is the way the boys who get these girls pregnant reacts.

Most of the time, the boy disappears or they want nothing to do with raising a child. Even the ones who may be forced to marry the girl, does not suddenly "put a man head on his body" and become responsible.

While I agree that there should be some tangible point one can reach or attain that would identify them as moving into the stage of manhood, sometimes this is not easily done.

However, I believe that there are certain things a teenage boy can do that will help him to prepare for manhood. Like I said earlier, manhood involves a certain mindset and a certain way one responds to life and the situations that may arise.

For instance, it takes a responsible boy to save money and prepare for a financial future. It takes a certain mindset to deny oneself of certain pleasure in the now to obtain a better result in the future.

In any event, no matter whether or not you agree with the various rites of passage discussed earlier, one of the important things to note about any of those events, as well as the Western version of rites of passage, every boy must prepare for that time.

Preparation – that will determine whether or not the boy makes that transition into manhood successful.

That's why I'm convinced that teenage boys who follow these simple steps will reach that point where they will find that they are mentally, emotionally and spiritually prepared for transitioning into the stage of manhood.

Consider following these steps as your Rites of Passage into manhood.

Warning – Choose Your Friends Carefully!

"My son is a good boy, with a good heart, who made a terrible mistake….he got caught up with the wrong company which caused him to make a bad decision."

With those words read before a courtroom, a mother pleaded for her son, before the judge sentenced him to 30 years in prison. Her son was sentenced with another boy (who got life in prison) for the beating death of a homeless person.

It was a friendship that turned out to be deadly.

A father held his head in shock and tears rolled down his face as police officers told him that his son was involved in a robbery that claimed the life of two people. The heartfelt cry of a father sounded as if he was in mourning for his dead.

All the father could do was hold his head and ask "Why? Why? Why?"

It was later revealed that hanging out with the wrong crowd led to this boy spending the rest of his life in prison. No, he was not the gunman, nor did he actually commit the robbery, but he was with the boys who did and because he was placed at the scene of the crime, with his friends who committed the crime, he suffered the same fate which they suffered.

The stories are plentiful and familiar of people who made the wrong friendships and ended up paying the price. Their final remarks are one of disbelief and confusion. For the most part they led straight forward, ordinary, and in some cases great lives, but getting caught up with the wrong crowd or the wrong friends caused all the good they've been brought up under to go down the drain.

That's why this is the first step I want you to consider as you prepare to move into manhood - a warning to you to always choose your friends carefully.

Why is this such a big deal? Well, as you can see from the stories above, and even from stories that you may know personally, the wrong kinds of friends can sabotage any possibility of living a great life.

Yeah, I know you consider your friends to be your boys, the life of the party and the people you hang out with, all of that is well and good, but if these friends of yours have a tendency to get caught up in negative behavior, you may never live long enough to see manhood.

Or worse, you may have to live out your manhood days behind prison bars. All because you did not take seriously the need to choose the right kinds of friends.

To you this step may sound kind of lame because you just can't see how your friends can prevent you from becoming the kind of man you would like to be.

This warning is to help prevent you from sabotaging your life now.

I've seen so much potential lost, destinies destroyed and hope of a better life thrown out of the window because of the wrong kinds of friends.

If the stories you know about the results of friendships gone bad are not enough warning to you, then perhaps learning from someone who has more experience about life than you do may do the trick. This step in making a successful transition from a boy to a man is so serious that it is something which King Solomon warned his son about. In Proverbs 22:24-25 says "Do not make friends with a hot-tempered man; do not associate with one easily angered, or you may learn his ways and get yourself ensnared."

Wow! That's straight forward.

Solomon wasn't being prejudiced against anyone, but he was warning his son about how to choose his friends. He knew that bad company corrupts good morals and so he warned his son against keeping bad company.

The same warning I'm offering to you.

Telling kids to avoid bad company is like talking to kids who live in utopia, a make believe place where everything is perfect.

The truth is warning teenagers about watching the company they keep seems to be an exercise in futility. That's because teenagers believe they know everything there is to know about life and therefore have the right to choose their own friends.

However, take it from someone who has been around a lot longer than you have – choose your friends carefully. The wrong friendships can leave you in a place where you would not like to be.

You should know that friendship is a word that is thrown around too loosely and for the most part people have no idea what a true friend really looks like. Here's some advice, a friend (a true friend) is someone who has your best interest at heart.

Anytime you have a "friend" who encourages you to get involved in negative behavior or who encourages you to break the law, that person is not your friend and to continue hanging around that person will lead to your eventual destruction.

In fact, those who are bent on doing wrong are placed in a category as one of the things the Bible says God hates.

In Proverbs 6:16-19, the warnings are so clear cut: "There are six things the Lord hates, seven that are an abomination to him; haughty eyes, a lying tongue, hands that shed innocent blood, a heart that devises wicked schemes, feet that are quick to rush into evil, a false witness who pours out lies and a man who stirs up dissensions among brothers."

Out of those seven things that the Lord hates, Solomon pointed out *hands that shed innocent blood, a heart that devises wicked schemes, feet that are quick to rush into evil, a false witness who pours out lies and a man who stirs up dissensions among brothers.*

All of these are characteristics of someone who spells trouble. That's the kind of person to avoid when choosing your friends.

You ever had those "friends" who were quick to suggest that you go and do something that you knew was wrong? Then they start calling you names when you decide not to go along with them and do that thing. Trust me, those people are not your friends.

A true friend is one who seeks to help you become the best you can be. They're there to listen to you and offer positive, sound advice. A friend is someone who is there through the good and the bad times. They focus on your strengths and help you through your weaknesses. They never, ever put you down, degrade you or make you feel less than a person. True friends help you achieve your goals and if you fall short they offer words of encouragement.

Yes, and true friends are the kind of guys you want to hang out with.

Proverbs 17:17 says that a friend loves at all times.

In other words, when you're up or when you're down; when you have money or when you're broke; when you're nice and even when you're having a bad day – a friend will love you in spite of what's happening in your life.

Let me point out this fact – friendship is a two-way street.

In other words anytime you find yourself involved in a friendship (or even a relationship) where you're the only one giving, encouraging or the only one going out of your way to help the other person, then you must evaluate that relationship and decide whether or not that person is truly your friend.

I've had those friendships where the guys were always at my house, eating up my food, playing with my games and I never saw their homes, met their parents or ate in their kitchens nor played with any of their games.

It turned out that those guys were never really my friends, but were using me. I found that out when I brought it to their attention that they were always at my house. They got angry and left and I never really heard from them again. Of course, at the time I was hurt by that because I thought I had lost my friends, but time eventually revealed that they were never really my friends.

If I had known Proverbs 19:6, back then I would not have been so hurt. It says "Many curry favor with a ruler, and everyone is a friend of a man who gives gifts."

In other words, as long as you have to give, those fake friends will always stick around. But the minute you don't have it to give them, they're gone like yesterday's news.

Ask kids involved in gangs how they got there and you will discover the basic reason was the need to feel wanted. That's why a guy who doesn't really know the people in the gang would still be willing to lay down his life for the members of the gang, simply because they made him feel wanted and needed. They made him feel like he was a part of a family.

Proverbs 18:24 says "A man of many companions may come to ruin, but there is a friend who sticks closer than a brother."

Don't be eager to have lots of friends. Some guys think that's cool, but Proverbs says it can lead to ruin. More friends can mean more problems. Jesus, when he walked the earth had many people follow him on a daily basis, but only 12 he choose to be in his inner circle.

Out of those 12 only three he deemed close – Peter, James and John. They were the only ones involved in Jesus' intimate, personal circumstances of his life. You should consider taking the same approach.

That brings me to something else you must be careful of – that is peer pressure.

Peer pressure is the pulling one feels from a group of his peers to do certain things he knows may be wrong. The pressure will come from those "friends" who may be urging you on and encouraging you to do the wrong thing.

For instance, your "friends" may be urging you to steal something out of the store and call you names if you insists on not doing it. Being called names like "punk", "soft", "scary cat", "wimp" or "loser" are some of the phrases that are used to try and get someone to do something that is wrong.

I used to hang out with what was considered the "bad boys" of the neighborhood. Of course I was just a teenager (between the ages of 13-16) and never thought they were "bad boys". Sure, I knew they did some things that didn't sit well with me, but as far as I was concerned they were my "friends".

Two of the things they did that did not sit well with me were the fact that they could cuss the paint off a wall and they were thieves. Besides those two things I thought they were cool. That was until they tried to get me to go somewhere and steal something with them.

We were fine up to that point.

I don't know how, but I remember that day. We had just come from the beach and were hanging out when one of the guys had this idea to go and steal some electronics from a neighbor's house. I told them I was not going and they called me all of the mean things they could think of, in their attempt to try and urge me to go with them.

But deep inside, I knew it was wrong (because my mother always told me that stealing was wrong) and so I made a tough decision to go home instead of going with them. It was hard to get up and leave them there and go home, but I knew I didn't want to do what they wanted me to do.

Of course, they went ahead with their plan and succeeded too.

The next day they bragged about their accomplishment and of course they continued to call me all the bad names they could think of. We continued to hang out together for a while, but every time they made a decision to go and steal something they would try and get me to go with them, but I would always decline and go home.

And every time I did, I would have to hear the mean names they would call me. They were putting on the peer pressure.

But eventually the message got through – I was not going to go stealing with them. So, over time they would not even tell me about their plans to go and steal things, they would wait until I went home and went and did what they wanted to do.

A lot of it was petty thievery, but it eventually led to them stealing bigger items and they became involved in more daring attempts. Needless to say, many of them ended up in jail for stealing, one even went away for murder.

I always think back on those times and wonder where I would be today if I had buckled under their peer pressure and went along with them. No doubt, I have my mother to thank for instilling in me certain values, which kept me through those tough adolescent times.

That's what I'm attempting to do to you – instill some principles which I hope you will take with you through those tough adolescent times in your life and eventually into manhood.

Always do what you know to be right, no matter what.

If you ever get caught up with the wrong crowd and you feel they're putting pressure on you to do what you feel is wrong, always, always walk away first and clear your head. If you stay, the pressure will so overwhelm you and you will not think straight. Get away and think about what they are asking you to do and see if it lines up with what you have been taught, and then make a decision.

Or ask some adult whom you trust and have confidence in to give you sound advice.

Never make a decision while under peer pressure.

However, if you make a conscious decision to choose the right kind of friends, then maybe you could avoid being put under pressure by your peers.

Choosing The Right Career Path

Okay, now that you've made a conscious decision to choose your friends carefully, the second step that will help to prepare you for the path of manhood is choosing the right career.

There is no better time to begin thinking about a career than in your early teens. Although this may not seem like a big deal to you right now, believe me, once you begin to think about your career now, you will be ready for when the time comes for you to choose a college.

Your college choice will no doubt be based on what it is you have decided you want to be in life.

Do you know what it is you would like to be? Is there a career you always had in your mind and concluded that when you "grow up" you're going to be that?

You see, the career you choose will determine, in a sense the kind of life you will live as you grow into manhood.

This is something which many people have great regrets about. Listen to them talk and you would hear the cry of regret on their lips as many reveal how because they did not set their heart on a career, now they are stuck in a job they hate.

Most people do not deliberately choose a career, they just kind of go on whatever talent or gift they have and wing it from there. That is one of the biggest mistakes you can make. Think about it, if you don't make a choice of what it is you want to be once you leave college, then life will kinda make the choice for you. And you may not necessarily like the choice life makes for you.

But the good thing is you have the power to make that choice.

Many schools, especially high schools, would hold what they call "Career Day" events, during which time representatives from various professions, companies and businesses would set up booths in the high school gym and the senior students are released into the gym to go from one booth to the next to find out information about the companies, professions and businesses represented.

The objective was to give senior high students some idea of the variety of careers that are available once they finish college. Now, with the internet, not that many schools hold these "career days" anymore. It's not really necessary, because you can now go on line and find out all the information you need about any field of career.

I know, as a teenage you feel invincible, that you know it all and you feel that because you're young, you still have plenty of time to think about that stuff once you get out of school. How wrong you can be about that.

Time goes by quickly, and before you know it, one day you will look up and find yourself graduating from college and facing the age-old question of "what am I going to do with my life?"

Before you know it, your high school and college days will be over and you will be forced into the real world. Are you ready for that?

Too many teens find themselves with no college options, no career goals, and so once they leave high school they begin the cycle of bouncing from job to job, with no real purpose, goals or ambition.

Making a conscious decision now on what it is you would like to have as a career can help you to avoid those pitfalls.

Do you know what it is you want to be in life? Is it a clear picture in your mind, or are you still juggling a few options? If you still have a few ideas up in the air, that's fine as long as you narrow down those options before you graduate high school.

Going into college with a defined purpose helps make choosing your major a whole lot easier. Whenever I speak to teens about making a decision on their career goals they are quick to point at some movie stars, musicians, rappers, singers or business people who never went to college, yet became successful.

Yes, there are lots of people who are successful who never even finished high school nor went to college, but those are the exception and not the rule. There is no guarantee that your life will follow that same path. Are you willing to take that chance and just sit back and let life happen to you?

As a teenager, the prospect of bouncing around from one odd job to the next may seem okay for a while, even exciting to a point, but there will come a point in time when you will have to know what it is you want to be in life and go after it with every fiber of your being.

The problem with going from one job to the next is that you could end up on one of those odd jobs for the rest of your life, and hate every minute of it.

Choosing the right career will determine whether you live like a king or whether you live like a pauper once you become a man. It will have an impact on your love life, your marriage and your family life.

But what exactly is the "right" career?

This is always the hardest question, and one most teenagers, getting set to go into their final senior class asks themselves and others on a regular basis. Depending on who you ask, you will get various answers – some that make sense and some that can do nothing but send a blind teenager down the wrong path.

But the main idea is to ask. Ask as many questions as you can about different careers.

Find out what each one does, the amount of hours they work, how much that field is needed in your particular community or state, what's the pay scale, how long will it take to achieve the top position in any particular field, and most importantly, is it something that you can do and enjoy at the same time.

Little children constantly change what it is they say they want to be when they grow up. In fact, it would change from week to week. Some days you will hear a five year old say he wants to be a policeman, then some days you will hear him say that he wants to be a fireman, another time, it would probably be a lawyer, a doctor or even a dancer.

We expect that from little children, but as a teenager, you should be at a point where you begin to narrow down your options.

Now that you're grown, are you still stuck in the phase of short-term aspirations? Are you a senior in college and still not sure what it is you want to pursue as a career? That will lead to frustration and before you know it, you will be graduating college and still have no idea what it is you would like to be for the rest of your life.

Here is a bit of advice for you, especially those in the valley of decision.

First of all, if you haven't figured this out by now, let me make it plain – You should always choose a career and don't just look for a job. A job is something you can find anywhere, and most of the time, it's something that almost anyone can do. Jobs come and go, but a career can last a lifetime.

Of course, you will go through those years where you will get "odd" jobs during the summer breaks, or even while you're in school, but never think of those jobs as your final destination (unless of course, the job is in line with your future goal for a career).

Use these jobs to learn how to work with people, to enhance your skills, to deal with money and learn how to set a budget.

Working small jobs as a teenager goes a long way in helping you to develop as a person. Because most jobs require you to work with others, these jobs can help you develop your communication and leadership skills. They also help you learn a lot about people in general and the different personalities that exist in the work place and in the world.

Let me encourage you to never limit yourself to just one area while working on a job. If where you work have various levels of operation, although you may not consider that job to be your final destination, you should still be determined to learn about every area of operation on that job.

Watch people, ask questions and never waste time. This will help you to become a valuable employee.

Why is this important? Have you ever noticed that when there is a recession and companies begin cutting jobs, for the most part, some of the first people to be cut are those who specialize and can only do one job or operate in one capacity?

Those who have the skills to work in a number of areas are considered keepers. After all, the law of finance and business suggests that being able to pay one employee to do the job of three employees is common sense.

So never adopt the mindset of "that's not my area, so I'm not interested in learning about it." That's the wrong way to think. On every job you take, strive to not only be the best at what you do, but to become an asset to that business. Become a valuable employee.

Even when you find your career path, adopt the same mindset.

That's why your career must be something you enjoy.

History has proven that many people have chosen a particular career with just the financial rewards in mind, but never enjoyed a day of work. They go to work hating every moment, but with just the thought of the amount of money they make as their motivating force.

Don't get me wrong, money means a lot when it comes to choosing the right career, but what's the sense in making lots of money and fail to have the ability to enjoy it? If you can find a career that you enjoy and it pays you well, then God is with you and you are truly blessed; not many people can say that.

Let me point this out, if you decide to choose a career knowing full well that it's not a good paying career, then you had better make up your mind to have a hard time in life. The Bible says that money answers all things in the earth. But as long as you know where you stand financially and that you enjoy what you do, then you are free to make your choice.

How do you decide? Here's a suggestion - Because your career could possibly be the thing that you do for the rest of your working life, you had better choose something that you enjoy doing and something that pays well.

There are some careers that require you punch a clock, but they still pay well and they can be very fulfilling, but there are some careers that can give you freedom as well as a good paycheck. The options are so vast that you should begin at a young age considering exactly what it is you would like to do for the rest of your life.

Never ever, get caught up in a job or a career that you hate. Going someplace you hate and having to be there for eight hours or more each day, is the hardest thing in the world to do.

Another thing you must consider when choosing a career is look at the gifts (talents) that you have. What gifts have God blessed you with? You will know your gifts and talents when you do something that comes easy to you. It's something you can do without having to try hard or having studied it.

A gift can be musical, creative, analytical, or you may be good with your hands in fixing things. They are all gifts and for the most part, I believe that we are all born with certain gifts and talents. Some people may have more gifts than others, but everyone has at least one thing they're good at.

You must find your gift. When you do, you will be well on your way to finding your place in this world.

You see, God blessed you with certain gifts and talents to be a blessing to the world. Someone, somewhere needs what you have, that's why you must enhance your gifts as you grow up.

The Bible says that a man's gift shall make room for him and put him before Kings (Proverbs 18:16). I pray that your gift does that for you.
But the secret is finding out what you're good at.
Your career is normally found in your gifting, but make sure that it's something that you have a passion for and it's something which you enjoy.
Passion is another quality to consider when choosing a career.
If you don't have passion for something you will not do your best at it. Passion is what gets you out of bed with a spring in your step each morning. Passion is what makes you drive to work singing and anxious to get there, because you know it's something that you enjoy doing. Passion helps you become the best at what it is you do.
The moment you lose passion for something, leave it alone.
Whatever career path you choose, always perform at your best. Never give a half-hearted effort and make up your mind to become the best in your chosen profession. If it means staying up late studying, missing a television program, cutting back on going out one night out of the week, strive to be the best at what you do.
Make your work place need you and not the other way around. Combine your gifts and talents with passion and an enjoyment for what it is you do and success cannot help but find you. The choice is up to you.
Don't forget, find out everything you can about a profession or a career you may be interested in. Talk to people who may be in the same profession. The more you know the better chance you have of making an intelligent choice.

Education is the Key

The kind of jobs you get and eventually the kind of career you follow will be determined by your level of education.
Yes, education is the key to becoming what it is you want to be in life. A lack of education will leave you with very few options.
You may be wondering why even put this chapter in this book because after all "everyone knows that you have to be educated". You would think that would be the case, but sadly it isn't. Statistics show that more and more kids are opting to drop out of school before completing high school.
This is especially true for boys, because statistics indicate that more boys have the tendency to be the ones to leave high school before they reach grade nine. I'm not sure what it is, but for some reason most boys hate school. Perhaps it has something to do with the fact that school requires one to sit and listen and comprehend, and boys, because of their restless nature would prefer to be out and about, playing or doing something else.
Yes, I know that more boys are good at building things and doing things with their hands and therefore they don't see the need for sitting in some classroom, listening to a teacher "drone on" about books and writing and learning.
I understand that and to some degree can agree with that, but even people who build things or construct things will need to have even the most basic of education, like knowing how to read, write and everyone must know how to add and subtract.
The bottom line is, education is a must, especially in order to compete in today's world, where information comes at you at an alarming rate. There is so much things to know these days that those who refuse to read and study will fall behind.
You have to take your education seriously if you desire to live a better life once you reach manhood.

Perhaps you know people who are "stuck" on jobs they hate, but they have no choice but to stay on those jobs because they have no other options. They all want better lives, but because of a lack of proper education, their choices for better jobs are limited, which in turn can mean that their earning power is limited.

You ever wonder why it appears that women are taking over the work-place. It's because girls are taught from a very young age that if they take their education seriously, do well in high school, go to college, excel and graduate, they can come out and get the kind of job they wish, and perhaps even demand their salary because of their qualifications.

Too often we never send the same message to guys. We leave guys to do as they please and too many parents are allowing boys to just drop out of school if they want to. But that's doing an injustice to our boys.

So, I'm sending the message to you, stay in school, do your best, excel, look forward to college and pursue it with all of your ability so that once you're done, you can enter the work place armed and prepared to demand your salary.

You can do it. Don't believe the lie that girls are smarter than boys. We all have a level of learning capacity (some more than others) and we all can apply ourselves to learning what we need to learn in order to be prepared.

Be disciplined in your studies and not get distracted by the call of the "party animals", who have no intentions on doing any work in school. That's the crowd that's going to lead you down the path which leads to a dead-end.

Think for yourself and not be so easily persuaded by other people.

Maybe some of the guys who lead the party bandwagon come from rich, wealthy families and whether they do well in school or not will not matter, because they will have their families' wealth to fall back on. Are you in the same position? Are you from a wealthy family and whether you succeed or not in school will not affect your inheritance? If you're not in that position, then you had better be wise and not follow the party crowd.

Guess what, you can still party as long as all of your school assignments are completed and as long as you know what you have to do to excel in school. That's using wisdom.

Studying can get tiresome and boring at times, but every time you feel that way just think about your future possibilities without a proper education. Think about being stuck on a dead-end job with no other options.

The good thing about school is, it's not forever.

Too many young people give up too easily, especially if they come across something that may seem difficult at the time. But school is not forever. It is just a phase in your life, although it is a very important phase and it will determine how you live once you become a man.

Consider this, there is nothing in this world you cannot be, as long as you're willing to discipline yourself to learning. Education opens so many doors, so many possibilities, but it's all up to you.

No one can make you learn. No one can really force you to go to school, so the decisions you make about education are the decisions that will affect your future.

There are people who are forced to go "back" to school and attend night classes, simply because they did not take the time they had in school seriously. They went out into the work force and realized that they could not compete because of a lack of proper education.

Think about the time they could be saving if they had done what they should have done while they were in school.

The age in which you live is called the "information age" and those who are not willing to seek out, study and apply that information will get left behind and will not be able to compete in the market place.

It's all up to you.

Education is one of the keys to success, but you will have to be willing to obtain the key and use it to open the many doors of opportunities that awaits you in the world.

The 'Golden Rule' – He Who Has The Gold, Makes The Rules

Perhaps one of the most defining aspects of manhood is being financially responsible and capable.
There is nothing more comforting to a family and attractive to a woman than a man who is financially stable. Women thrive on security and financial security is one of them. A woman can put up with a lot of shortcomings by a man but financial irresponsibility is not one of them.
In fact, being financially stable is one of the things that will help you stand tall as a man, because it shows that you have been responsible through your teen and early adult years. This may not seem like a big deal now, but taking control of your financial life will go a long way in helping you become the kind of man people will look up too.
In an earlier chapter we talked about choosing the right career, but even before you begin to function in your chosen field of a career, if you have the opportunity to work at "odd" jobs, knowing how to handle the money you make from those jobs will be critical.
By the way, if your plan is to spend every pay check you get because in your mind it really doesn't matter now what you do with your money, you will be in for a tough time once you step into manhood. You have to start now thinking differently about money, because you're gonna need a lot of it once you become a man.
The Bible says that "Money answers all things in the earth".
In other words, you will need money throughout your life, especially when you become a man. In fact, even as a teen you need money now, imagine when you become a man and take on responsibilities. How you view money will determine if you will have enough to take on some of the responsibilities of manhood.
Consider this for a moment, the only thing in this world that can stop someone from getting whatever he wants or going wherever it is he wants to go is a lack of money. Have enough money and there is nothing in this world that is manufactured or made that you cannot purchase or no place on God's green earth you won't be able to travel to.
Money, money, money, have enough of it and it can literally take you around the world. With money, you can buy whatever you want, go wherever you like and live the kind of life that most people only dream of living.
So, my advice to you is try to get as much money as you can. Work hard for it, use your talents and gifts to obtain it, and never, ever think that you're not good enough to have lots of it.
Look at the people who have lots of money, then look at those who don't have it, and you will see so many differences in the way they live. When you have lots of money, the possibilities for your life are endless.
I'm convinced that poverty is a curse. Not having enough money to do things, go places, buy stuff, or pay bills can leave you depressed, filled with regret and struggling to survive. Not having enough money could seriously affect your relationships.

There was a time in my life when I believed that poverty was Godly, because that's what I was taught and led to believe. I was told that rich people were never happy, they were hiding their sorrow behind their wealth and their things and they were certainly headed to hell.

Of course, I felt good about being poor, because after all, I was on my way to Heaven, and once I got there, it would be worth it all. Besides there's a mansion waiting for me there, right? But I soon came to realize that I was limited because my money was limited. I began to realize that what people told me about wealth and money was not true at all. Rich people didn't look sad to me. They didn't have time to be sad, they were too busy sailing off on their yachts, flying to exotic destinations in their private jets, driving around in their expensive cars, or too busy shopping to find time to be sad.

No, I'm convinced that poverty is a curse. There is no humility or benefit in being poor, broke, busted and disgusted. It's no fun having to go into the food store and not have enough money to buy the essential things to sustain your life.

That's why I encourage you to make as much money as you can and when you become rich, don't feel that you have to apologize about it.

Do it the right way

Now, before I'm branded as a goal digger, money hog or a materialistic person, or before you have a warped sense of money, let me stress this fact – while making money should be a goal, never cheat, steal or lie to get money. Never do anything that's against the laws of God or against the laws of the land to get money.

Why not do these things to obtain money? Because whenever you lie, cheat or steal, someone else is on the other side of those things and eventually what you do to someone else will come back to haunt you. Some people call it karma and some call it poetic justice, the Bible says what a man sows, he will reap.

Besides, do you realize that you don't have to be what some consider to be rich to be financially stable and financially independent? Being financially stable means you're not living from paycheck to paycheck. It means that you can pay all of your bills comfortably and still have something left over.

Let me clear this up quickly – when I encourage you to make as much money as you can, I warn you not to love money. Money is not something to use to oppress others or to make people do things they don't want to do. Money is not to love, but to use to meet your needs and the needs of others.

The Bible says that the LOVE of money is the root of all evil. (1Timothy 6:10) In other words, the minute you begin to love money, that is the time when you enter a dark, dark place from which you may not escape.

You should make your money the old fashioned way, through hard work. Yes, the infamous four letter word – WORK – it never killed anyone. At least, not that I know of. But hard work never goes out of style. Hard, honest work is one of the marks of a good man.

Proverbs 13:11 says "Dishonest money dwindles away, but he who gathers money little by little makes it grow."

Rest assured that hard work these days does not mean going into a field (unless that's your profession), but when I say hard work, I mean, if you're an accountant, be willing to work hard to earn your salary. Doctors work hard to make their money, although some may not think that they work as hard as someone in the construction field.

Once you've found your career path, be willing to work hard to not only be the best in your field, but to command your salary. Yes, you determine how much money you make.

Also, use your gifts and talents to make money. I'm convinced that every person born has at least one gift or talent inside of them that could make them rich here in this world, but many never discover that gift or talent and die in poverty and regret.

Your task will be to find you gifts and talents and find what ways are best (and honest) to put those gifts and talents to use to serve others. That will lead to financial prosperity. There's a saying that if you find a need and fill it, you will never want for anything in life.

That's what great inventors did; they found out what it was the world needed and they provided it as a service or a product, and unknowingly, they became rich by filling that need.

More money makes you more of what you already are

There is a saying that I heard years ago, which I could never forget. It goes like this "more money makes you more of what you already are." What does that mean? It means that money is an amplifier; it amplifies who you are inside.

That's why you find some really rich people who are popular and have prestige still feel empty inside and some even commit suicide. That's because if they were empty inside before they had money, more money left them feeling emptier inside. Yes, they may have been able to surround themselves with more people and more things, but not even that satisfied them.

If someone drinks a little alcohol as a broke person, the minute they become rich they can no longer just drink a little alcohol, but now they can become an alcoholic. Money makes you more of what you're already are.

While I'm advocating hard work, let me point out that you should never sacrifice your family, your relationship with God or your health in working hard to make money. Keep everything in balance. History is filled with those in the past (and even today) who were fooled into believing that they could have it all at the same time.

They wanted to have the great careers, be hard workers, working long hours, have the big houses, nice cars and checking privilege, as well as have a strong family life. It sounds like the ultimate dream, but very few actually achieve such a dream, at least on their own.

Only God can make that happen, and even God is one of balance. No, having it all is a gamble that no one through the ages have ever won.

You have to decide what is more important to you – the money, your career or your family.

LEARN ABOUT INVESTMENTS

Now that you know how important it is to have as much money as you can make in an honest way, you should be careful not to squander that money.

Squandering is being wasteful. Never spend all of your money on fast living, partying or on "friends" who are really leeches disguised as friends. No, I'm not saying you can't have fun and enjoy what you've worked so hard to obtain, but what I am saying is it would be sad to have worked so hard to make the money, only to throw it away by careless spending.

And believe it or not, money can actually run out, no matter how much of it you have. If you don't believe that, do a research on people who've won lotteries – millions of dollars at one time – and you will see that some of those people who just went out and spend, spend, spend, ended back up where they started – with nothing.

Imagine that, a person has $20 million (in some cases more) at their disposal and they end up broke.

How can that happen? Well, it's call squandering and not investing. Learning to invest not only helps you to spend your money wisely, but it helps your money make a return for you in the future. In other words, investments help secure your financial future. As you get older in age, with proper investments and a good possible return on your investments, you can retire from working early and enjoy your later years.

Yes I know, later years is not even close to your mind right now, but believe me, those years will come. And when they do, if you've taken heed to what I'm saying, those years will be even more exciting than your youthful years, because you will be able to do what you want, when you want. With a good financial foundation and accumulated wealth, you will be able to enjoy the lives of your kids and grand kids with ease.

The key thing to remember about investments is making proper investments. Not everything that has the word "investment" written on it is a real investment. Remember, there are con artists and schemers out there, waiting to take advantage of unsuspecting, eager to get rich people. Don't fall into that trap.

Learn as much as you can about finances and investments. There are lots of credible sources out there that can give you that kind of information, so read, read, read. Never tire of reading and taking in information. The more you know, the better chances of you being able to spot a fake a mile away.

Let me say, one thing I can suggest is always invest in real estate, apartments or condominiums and in companies that provide the basic necessities of life. Because when times get hard and consumers are unable to afford the finer things of life, they will always hold onto the things they consider necessary, like food, shelter and good health.

Of course, you should also consider investing in stocks and bonds and in Fortune 500 companies, but those types of investments should not be your first choice. Get a feel for investing first before you risk it all.

Consider buying a piece of property as your first investment. Having land puts you in a position to build good credit and it gives you a foot up on lending institutions. That land can be used as collateral for future investments.

Future investments like buying or building your own home should be your next step.

I cannot stress enough how important it is for you to have a goal of buying your own house at an early age in your life. This will cut down on you having to spend years and years renting someone's apartment and making them rich. Some people spend all of their lives renting an apartment and never owning a place of their own. Renting is really dead money and should never be considered a permanent situation.

A home is an investment that always accumulates in value as long as you take care of it. Make sure that it's in a neighborhood that's increasing in value and not in one that's already completed, run down and headed down in value. And always treat your home as your investment, because in essence it is.

A lot of people consider a car an investment, but the truth is, it's not. The minute you drive a brand new car off a lot, it begins to depreciate in value. A car is only good to you for the length of time it takes to repay the bank for it. Also, a car is only really worth something as long as it continues to work properly. The day it begins to break down and you find that you continually have to get it fixed, get rid of it.

Let me encourage you to consider not buying a new car your first time out. Contrary to popular belief, your first car does not have to be a new car. In fact, buying a car three or four years old, with not that many miles on it, will still give you the benefit of driving a nice car, but with little or no bank payments.

Buying a new car should be something you consider once you are established in your career.

Yes, Antique, Vintage cars are considered investments, but like the stocks and bonds, leave that kind of investment for when you've established yourself financially and feel more confident that you can handle making those kinds of decisions.
As the times change around you, continue to read and keep up to date with the financial markets, not just about the place in which you live, but keep up to date with the financial world around you.

SAVING SHOULD BE A PRIORITY
I cannot stress the importance of learning how to save.
This is something so many young people get very little information on that by the time they do get some idea of what saving is supposed to be about, they have already made a lot of bad money choices and developed a spending habit that has become addictive.
You should begin learning about saving from as early as possible.
A saving habit should begin from the very first time you begin getting an allowance. No matter how much it is you earn, never, ever spend all of your money. Always plan to put aside at least 10 percent (or more, if possible) of what you earn into a savings account.
Put it in a piggy bank, one which you're unable to get into until it's full and you're ready to break it open. Take that money and put it in the bank on your savings account and if you don't have a savings account, establish one with a good bank.
Each time you fill a piggy bank, and take that money and put it on your account, you will be putting something aside for your financial future. Always start your savings with a small amount from what you make, and don't try to save a huge hunk of what you make, because it can be a strain and you may get discouraged. If it is something you can take out and not feel like you're depriving yourself, you will begin to learn a saving habit.
Of course, as you get older and you begin to work odd jobs and make more money, you would want to consider putting even more aside in your savings account.
The point is, never consume all that you earn. If you do, you will end up living a broke adult life and always having to depend on someone else to take care of you. But as long as you have a steady savings account, you will always have money to sustain you, particularly in a time when you might need it.
If you make $10 for your allowance each week, try to save two dollars from that and put into your piggy bank. Once you're consistent with that each week, by the end of the month you would have saved eight dollars. Eight dollars each month and by the end of the year you would have saved $96.
That may not sound like much now, but imagine saving $96 from the age of 12 up until you reach 15 or 16, when you can begin to take on odd jobs outside of the home and begin putting aside even more. You could save a hefty amount even as a child.
Of course, like I said, once you begin to take on jobs outside of the home, you will be making more than $10 a week and therefore you can begin to save even more. For instance say you begin to make $100 a week and you save $20 from that 100, in one month you would have saved $100.
Multiply that by 12 (12 months in a year) and you would have saved $1,200 in a year.
Now, that sounds like even more money, doesn't it? Yes, imagine saving $1,200 each year, in five years you would have saved $6,000! Money that can be in the bank collecting interest.

The point is make saving a habit, as well as make it fun. Once you have saved so much money, never make a decision to spend all of your savings at one time. When the time comes to use money from your savings account, always leave something there to continue your saving process. But remember, the decision to use money from your savings account should be based on the importance of what you're purchasing.

If you don't have to touch your savings, then don't. Continue to add to it until you really need it. The whole idea behind saving is to build a financial future and not have to depend on others to take care of you. It's called being financially independent.

While I'm on the topic of saving, let me point out something very important in your financial future – learn to begin to tithe. A tithe is taking 10 percent of what you earn and putting into the church you attend.

Tithing is something ordained by God to ensure that the church is always in a position to help the poor and to take the gospel around the world. Tithing also helps you to recognize that God is first place in your life, especially when it comes to money. God always honors the tithe and has promised to open up the windows of Heaven and pour you out a blessing (Malachi 3:8-12). Also, you should be considerate of those less fortunate than you and be willing to give to those in need. Your giving should always be guided by your heart, so always have a willing and compassionate heart.

DEVELOP GOOD CREDIT

Good credit does not depend on how much money you have in the bank.

I know that may sound like a paradox, based on all I've just been telling you, but the truth is credit has very little to do with how much money you have, and everything to do with how you handle money and your responsibilities.

In other words, credit is based upon how well you pay your bills and how good your name is among financial institutions. Credit is based on whether or not you are a person of your word and on whether or not you do what you promise to do.

For instance, good credit is based on if you pay your bills on time. Does lending institutions have to always come looking for you for the money you promised to pay at the end of the month? Do you have creditors calling you up and harassing you? If you do then you don't have good credit.

Paying bills on time, paying loans on time, paying credit cards on time, all help to build good credit. Before a lending institution loan you a dime, they check with other financial institutions to see if you were good at paying your bills. They check to see if you're a man of your word.

If they find that you're always late with payments and always evade credit calls, then they may very well be hesitant in lending you any money, no matter how much of it you may have saved in the bank. If, on the other hand, they find that you pay your bills ahead of time, you pay more than you should on your credit cards, then they will be more than willing to give you a loan or allow you to credit something.

Having good credit will take you a long way in obtaining the kind of funding you need for a business, for a car, for a house….in other words, good credit is good for business and good for investments.

The bottom line is use common sense. Know that your hard work in your young years should not go to waste once you step into adulthood. Let these young years of hard work prepare your financial future for your older years when you may not be able to work as hard.

If you have plans on one day getting married, taking on the responsibilities of a wife and eventually having a family, let me warn you, you had better be in a good financial position. A family, a home, cars, etc. all require money and nothing can destroy a marriage quicker than a lack of money.

Before you take on the responsibility of taking care of someone else, make sure that you have placed yourself in a good financial position.

Remember, you live in a world that's not fair. There are the "haves" and the "have nots" and each of us live in one of those categories. The "have nots" go without and some live on the streets or live depending on others to take care of them. They desire things they know they would never have, because of a lack of money.

The "have nots" dream of a better life, but it's only a dream, because money is what makes such a dream a reality. You never want to be in the category of the "have nots".

Don't let anyone fool you and tell you that wanting to make lots of money is materialistic. Money may not literally make this physical world go around, but it can literally take you around the world – and you can do it in style!

Searching For Love – Dealing With The Dating Scene

I want you to read this chapter carefully.
As boys – males – impressing the opposite sex sometimes determines many of the things that we do. In fact, most of the decisions you make as a guy and the reasons behind why you may do most of the things you will do would be because of basically two things, money and sex. Or should I say money and girls?
Yes, guys always feel the need to impress the girls. It's just a part of our make-up.
There is really nothing wrong with that, except when we go overboard in an effort to impress, and we end up hurting someone else.
Never underestimate the power of love.
Like money, love can either make you happy, or the lack of it can leave you feeling alone, miserable and depressed.
But unlike money, love is harder to come by these days. Sure, some people use money to try and buy love, but the truth is, you can't buy love. If you could, it would be a cheap, counterfeit. You see, love is something that comes from the heart and soul.
For most people, love is something that's hard to explain. Some call it a good feeling, others call it a knowing deep down inside, and some have made the crucial mistake of inter-changing the word love with the word sex. The two are not the same thing.
Firstly, you should know that the reason why people have so many varied (even crazy) ideas about love is because they ignore the true source of love – which is God. The Bible says that God is love. That means love comes from God. He encompasses love. He doesn't have love, he IS love. So be weary of people who claim to love you, but they don't know or have God. Because God is love, it's very difficult to experience true love without him.
Thus the reasons for people linking love with feelings and sex.
True love goes beyond the two. You see feelings change, but love doesn't. Sex is mostly physical, while love is more of an emotional and a conscious decision. You don't think so, then how can you explain the fact that people who have "great sex" can still eventually separate and go their separate ways?
Sex does not connote love.
Everyone is searching for love. Even those people who call it something else, the bottom line is that we are all looking for love. Why? Because there is a void inside of us that only love can fill. Some have tried to fill that void with other things, but true love is the missing piece.
As a teenager or a young male, as you go through this life, you too will take that journey in search of love; simply because we were created to love and to be loved. It's a sad thing when people say that they can live life without love. Trust me, those are lonely, hurting people.
Okay, so you've reached that age where you're not only spending all of your brain power thinking about girls, but you feel you're ready to begin dating girls. Dating and relationships can be one of the most painful experiences you will ever go through, or it can be one of the most thrilling, memorable experience you will ever have.
How you deal with relationships in your youth will have an impact on you once you become a man.
As you begin to date and get into relationships, let me warn you again to guard your heart with all diligence.

Don't be quick to give your heart to someone, unless you know exactly how they feel about you. There is nothing more painful than loving someone who doesn't love you back. It's an exercise in futility, and you're setting yourself up to be used and to get hurt.

You guard your heart by watching who you let inside of it. If you haven't figure this out by now, you will as you live each day – that is the fact that there are some cruel, mean people in the world. Not everyone will mean you good and some people will take your heart and crush it. Be careful of letting that happen.

People will be quick to say "I love you", but may not even have a clue of exactly what that means. Some people may be sincere, but may be operating out of feelings alone. Others, as I said before, will use those words to pull you into a snare (a trap).

While most teenagers are convinced that they feel "true love" for each other, the truth is, they are operating in puppy love and that kind of love takes time to mature. Puppy love is innocent and we all go through it, but never think that puppy love is ultimate love, because it isn't. Puppy love knows nothing about sacrifice or compromise, it only cares about its own feelings.

You may be wondering, well, how will I know if someone really loves me? Well, first of all, let me say this, Love is a verb! What do I mean? Well, because words come so easily for some people, it may be hard to tell if someone really mean what they say. But the good thing with love is, it's an action.

A person can tell you they love you a hundred times a day, but if their actions do not reflect what they say, then, it's only lip service, and in that case, you should run as fast as possible from that person. Don't even look back.

You see when someone loves you they show it in their actions. Love can't help but express itself through action. A person in love will do small (and big) things to demonstrate how they feel. Simple things like calling you just to check up on you and see how you're doing; they may express that love with little gifts for no special reason; a card wishing you a great day, preparing you lunch or dinner, purchasing your favorite CD or DVD when it comes out, or hugging you for no reason, but to show you love. Showing love can be as or simple as writing you a note to say how much they appreciate you.

All of these are just some of the ways a person can express their love. There are so many other ways, but true love has to express itself through action. The Bible says that God so loved the world that he GAVE his only Begotten Son (John 3:16). You see, love gives, love does, love is a verb.

How can someone claim they love you and the only time you hear from them is when you call them? If you're the only person in the relationship buying gifts to express your love, or doing simple things to express how you feel, then watch out, you could be caught up on a one-way street.

Yes, I know that there are people who can pretend to do these things to try and convince you that they love you, but if their heart's not sincere, it won't last long. How long do you think a wolf can hide in sheep's clothing? Not long, because the wolf has to express its true nature, eventually.

That's why relationships are time tested. They're not rushed. Anyone can pretend for a few days or a few weeks, but eventually, the real person leaks out as time wears on.

That brings me to my next point – a guideline to finding the right girl to date and the right woman to marry.

Okay, I know this may not be something that you will want to hear right now, but trust me, this kind of information will be priceless to you as you grow and mature.

No, no one can tell you who to marry, but I just want to offer some guidelines that may help you in your selection process through the years.

First of all you should know that boys and girls (men and women) are different and view life differently. Not only are they different physically, they are different emotionally and mentally. They view life in two totally different ways.

For the most part, because girls are more emotional than boys, they enter relationships on a wave of emotions. Boys view relationships differently, focusing more on physical attraction than anything else.

Girls tend to enter relationships more seriously because of their emotional nature. Never, ever take advantage of that emotional need in a girl. It makes them vulnerable and if you approach such a girl in a half-hearted way, or with no intent on being serious, it can lead to a nasty relationship which could end in a bad break-up.

I should warn you that contrary to popular belief, dating is not a time for you to see how many girls you can have sex with. In fact, sex should not even be a factor during your dating years, because of all the implications and complications that comes with introducing sex into a friendship.

The purpose of dating is to foster a relationship or friendship. It's to get to know the other person – their likes and dislikes, their family history and their hopes for the future.

Too many people spend their time on dates just staring up in each other's faces and admiring each other's personalities. They never really get to know the other person. By the way dating also helps with your social skill.

People spend dating time being intimate and not asking questions about the other person. They're too much "in love" to use common sense. They want to spend all of their time together looking into each other's eyes and expressing how much they love each other.

When you begin dating a girl whom you think you may be seriously interested in, observe how she relates to members of her family, how her family relates to her and how they all relate to each other. Are her parents casual or "social" drinkers? How do her parents and her family deal with problems? What are her family's medical history? Is the family blood line prune to have heart disease, kidney disease or cancer running in it?

Observe how this girl treats her friends and how they treat her. Do they consider her a confidential and honest friend? Does she say one thing to her friends in front of their faces and say another thing behind their backs? Does she have a problem with cleaning her room or her apartment? When she do clean, does she spend the majority of that time complaining about having to do it, or does she do it with a positive attitude? Does she cook, and is she good at it? You may be thinking, why is all of that important?

You're just interested in the way this girl looks and in your mind that's all that matters.

Having all of these questions answered in your mind is critical because if you end up in a long term relationship with this person, whatever issues she have and whatever issues exist in her family, you will have to deal with, so it's best to know in advance, than to be surprised when it shows up.

Of course, you don't approach a date as if you're having a job or television interview. You want to be discreet with your questions and try to bring them up in normal conversations.

There are certain things someone will say if you only listen, and you may not have to ask all of those questions.

Then if you only be observant when you visit her at her home you can tell how she relates to her family and how they relate to her.

Remember, there is no such thing as "the perfect woman"; such a woman does not exist. We all have our faults and shortcomings, so don't be judgmental about anyone. But once there is honest communication between the two of you, it will go a long way in helping to establish a healthy relationship.

Let me warn you of this, when it comes to dating, prepare to have your heart broken.

I know, that's not something you want to hear and of course you intend to take every precaution to avoid being hurt, but trust me, when it comes to boys, girls, dating and matters of the heart, you can be sure that hurt will be involved.

That's just the nature of building relationships.

When those hurtful times hit you, always ask God to heal your heart and to help you to forgive. Forgiveness actually helps with the healing process. Know that being hurt by a girl is not the end of the world. It may feel that way, but believe me, life goes on.

When you're hurt it seems like that's all you can see, that's what makes it difficult for some people to move on. But if you can somehow look beyond your pain, you will see that time heals all wounds and eventually, you will be able to move on.

Take a broken heart in stride, knowing that the pain always passes.

In your pursuit of friendships, and relationships, one of which will eventually lead to your life long partner and wife, let me encourage you to always seek to have relationships with girls who share the same Faith as you.

Why is that such a big deal? If a girl loves God more than she loves you, all of the love she has for you will come out of her relationship with her Heavenly Father.

Love that has its roots planted in the Creator of Love will be built on a strong foundation. Of course, I'm not suggesting that once in a relationship the two of you will never have arguments or disagreements, but if you have the right foundation it can go a long way in helping both of you deal with those times of disagreements.

Well, once you are aware of the fact that boys and girls view relationships differently, it will determine how you approach relationships and how you approach girls. It could give you some guidelines in how you enter relationships. This information can help guide you in the way you speak to girls, how you handle their emotional nature and how you search for true love.

There have been too many young girls and boys, who date at an early age and by the time they're 14 or 15, they've already had sex, because they feel they're in love. Trust me, boys and girls at that age know very little about life, how can they possibly know about love?

Sex is not love and too many teenagers, especially girls, make that mistake. They feel that once they give a guy sex, then its evidence that they love him. Wrong. True, sex is an expression of love, but love, sex and relationships are for the mature.

There's no need to rush into an intimate relationship just because everyone else is doing it.

You should also consider having a serious relationship with a girl who encourages you, who motivates and pushes you to be a better person.

It's amazing what a woman can bring out of a man. Women push men to do things that they once may have considered impossible. The things a man would do for the love of a woman is beyond human comprehension.

Seek out a girl who brings the best out of you. Seek out a girl who is compassionate, who is considerate of others and who has a caring heart.

That sounds simple, but there are many girls who do not possess such qualities. Your task will be to find such a girl. But trust God to lead you to the right person for you.

Where does physical beauty come in? Well, that will be based on your preference and what it is you like in a girl. But what I'm talking about are matters of the heart and character – these are more lasting than mere physical beauty, which is fleeting.

I know that what I'm saying may go against everything your society is telling you, but trust me, attend to my words and you will live. If today's society is so right on their take on relationships, then why are there so many broken hearts and homes? Why are so many young people falling victims to sexually transmitted diseases, depression and suicide?

Avoid the loose woman

There is another side to this love thing I must tell you about and that is I feel obligated to warn you about a particular kind of woman which would be in your best interest to avoid. That is the "Bad woman". The Bible calls her the "adulterous" or the "loose" woman.

Those kinds of women can ruin a man's life.

There was once a Caribbean song which went something like this "bad woman cause good man sleep in policeman hand".

In other words a bad woman can cause a good man to end up in jail, just by the things she does, even by the words she speaks.

You say is there such women in the world, and the answer is yes and she can destroy a man faster than you can say "where's my life?" She can destroy your career, your marriage, your character and even your bank account.

Proverbs chapter five has much to say about such a woman. Remember, Solomon had hundreds of women, so if he says this kind of woman exist, then he should know. In chapter 5:3-6 he said "for the lips of a loose woman drip honey as a honeycomb and her mouth is smoother than oil; but in the end she is bitter as wormwood, sharp as a two-edged and devouring sword. Her feet go down to death, her feet take hold of Sheol (the place of the dead), she loses sight of and walks not in the path of life; her ways wind about aimlessly, and you cannot know them."

Solomon goes on in verse eight to warn his son to let his life be far from such a woman and to not even let his feet go near her house. That's how dangerous this kind of woman can be.

But it gets worse.

In chapter 6:24-26 Solomon again warns his son to embrace discipline so as to "keep him from the evil woman, from the flattery of the tongue of a loose woman. Lust not after her beauty in your heart, neither let her capture you with her eyelids. For on account of a harlot a man is brought to a piece of bread and the adulteress stalks and snares the precious life of a man."

It amazes me how a man can have a relationship with a bad woman and never see it. (The same way a woman can have a bad relationship with a man and never see it). No matter how much his friends talk to him and warn him about her, he cannot see anything wrong with her. Have you ever had a friend in that predicament? No matter what you and your other friends tell him about this girl, he just can't see what you guys are making noise about. He is blinded by love and even more frightening, he is held captive by her sexual vices. He's in a trap he cannot see, because she has blinded him.

That's the hardest kind of relationship to be in, because you're going down a path that leads to destruction and you're doing it with your eyes wide open. This guy in this trap believes everything this woman says, even though to others it's plain to see what she's doing.

She can go missing when she is supposedly on her way to see him, but when he asks her about her whereabouts, she always has a "justified" answer.

Even if she's flirty, he cannot see it. In fact, he thinks that's cute and it may be one of the attributes that attracted him to her. The only problem is, she's flirting in front of his face and with his friends. Shouldn't that be a signal that something is wrong? It should, but because he's blinded, he cannot see that.

A guy like that can only learn the hard way and he has to get hurt really, really bad by this woman before he can see her for who she really is. In some cases, I've known guys who actually caught their girlfriend in bed with another guy and although he was angry, he eventually forgave the girl and begged her to continue the relationship.

Isn't that crazy? But that's the power of a bad woman.

Solomon says that to follow the path of such a woman will cause a man to waste his years and his strength. It can even lead to death by some sexually transmitted disease.

"And you groan and mourn when your end comes, when your flesh and body are consumed." (Proverbs 5:11)

Solomon says all of this will happen because his son refused to listen to instructions. Don't let that be your cry. Listen to this advice and be wise.

Solomon goes on to encourage his son to be committed to his own wife and let her alone satisfy his sexual and emotional needs.

"Confine yourself to your own wife, let her children be for you alone and not the children of strangers within you. Let your fountain of human life be blessed with the rewards of fidelity and rejoice in the wife of your youth." (Proverbs 5:17-18)

I like what he asked in verse 20 "Why should you, my son, be infatuated with a loose woman, embrace the bosom of an outsider and go astray?"

What's so ironic about Solomon saying that is the fact that the majority of his wives and concubines were not from the land of Israel. In other words, Solomon was known for marrying "strange" women, many of whom caused him to forsake the way of his God and follow after foreign gods.

But because Solomon knew the price he paid for doing that, he is now in a position to sternly warn his sons about doing the same thing. In verse 21 he concludes "For the ways of man are directly before the eyes of the Lord, and He (who would have us live soberly, chastely and godly) carefully weighs all man's goings."

Do Not Awaken Love Before Its time

"Hormone Hurricane", that's what the older folks used to call us "out of hand" and "out of control" teenagers. At first it sounded as if it was a put down, but the truth is, they said it out of experience and out of concern for what they knew we were headed for during those turbulent teenage years.

At first, we just ignored the comment, partly because we really didn't know what it meant, also, because we really didn't care what it meant. We were teenagers and we were full of life. The world was before us and we were going to experience as much of it as we could.

It was a "take no prisoner" mindset.

It wasn't until some of us found ourselves in some serious predicaments with the opposite sex, that some of us began to ponder what the "old folks" were talking about when they called us "Hormone Hurricane".

It was simply this, as teenagers, your hormones are alive and become so active that they seem to be the driving force in almost every decision a teenager makes. That's why they called it a hurricane, because those hormones were raging, especially during the beginning of the teenage years.

That was then, and even today things have not changed. Teenagers will be teenagers no matter what year or no matter where they are. A teenager's hormones begin raging during their early teenage years and because some teenagers are not sure what's happening to them, they respond to situations and to other people in different ways, sometimes in a negative way.

Those same hormones cause teenagers not to only act out, but it increases their sexual awareness.

It's amazing when boys are very young, they think girls are "yucky", but by the time they reach 12 or 13, they begin to see girls in a whole new way.

That's when the hurricane begins to brew.

That is where life becomes very difficult and tricky.

Because those hormones seem to be in control, teenage boys (for the most part) can get sexually out of control. It's like dogs in heat. It seems like a feeling that is totally beyond your control. Most guys don't understand what they're going through and unless there is someone they can speak to, they tend to fall prey to those "misunderstood" and "heated" feelings.

But let me warn you, in the midst of all the confusion and heated feelings, do not awaken love before it's time.

These words were spoken by the man who was said to be the wisest man who ever lived, King Solomon. Not only was he wise in words of wisdom, but Solomon knew what he was talking about when it came to women, love, and sex, considering he had 700 wives and 300 concubines (or girlfriends).

Obviously, Solomon may have been considered the wisest man who ever lived, but to me, it was not a smart move to have 1,000 women. It is tough having to deal with one, imagine 1,000! As you grow, and become involved in relationships and friendships with girls and women, you will know that one woman is more work than any man can handle.

But there was great truth in what Solomon warned his son about when he told him "do not awaken love before its time" (Songs of Solomon 2:7). Why? Because once you awaken love before you're prepared to deal with it, it can destroy you.

What exactly does it mean not to awaken love before its time? It simply means do not arouse those sexual feelings inside of you before you are ready to deal with the results of sexual intercourse.

I'm sure you've seen (or may have been there yourself) teenage boys and girls become involve in friendships that quickly turn into intimate relationships. Of course, being young and immature, the relationship, for the most part, does not last and they "break-up".

Depending on who was the driving force behind the break up, the one who is "dumped" is devastated emotionally and mentally and sometimes even become physically sick.

Why? Because they were not ready to deal with the emotional roller coaster of a relationship, especially one that has taken on an intimate aspect.

You see, relationship and love are highly emotional aspects of life and those who are not prepared for it always find themselves scarred by a relationship that goes bad. Have you ever seen some men and women suffer from mental illness because of a relationship that went bad? That's the kind of bearing a relationship can have on one's mental and emotional state.

It can leave the mind so fragile, that it has the potential to snap at any moment.

When you let your heart become involved in an intimate and emotional relationship at an early age, you're setting yourself up for a fall.

I've seen kids at the ages of 12, 13, 14, 15 and 16 get involve in boyfriend, girlfriend relationships.

Sure, it starts off exciting because it's puppy love which is exciting in the beginning, but as soon as issues of life and the demands of a "relationship" sets in, what started out with lots of laughter and sweet words, quickly turns into anger and harsh words.

By then it's too late, because they've become emotionally and mentally involved, and so leaving or "breaking up" leaves each individual with scars, which they will carry for the rest of their lives. Those emotional scars go with them from one relationship to the next, each time, building up more and more hurt as each relationship falls apart.

Imagine if this kind of see-saw relationship begins at the tender age of 13, by the time you're in your 20s or 30s, you're one big ball of emotional and mental hurt from the past, and you will eventually explode. Sometimes the consequences can be fatal.
All because love was awaken before its time.
Can you imagine, just close friendships between boys and girls which ends badly can leave emotional and mental scars, so imagine when sex is thrown in the mix!
Let no one fool you, sex is a powerful, powerful force and if it's entered into at a stage in your life when you're not ready to handle it, it can literally destroy you. It's like putting a hand grenade into the hands of a four year old.
He doesn't know what to do with it, or even what it is. He can pull the pin out of the grenade, unaware of the danger he suddenly placed himself (and everyone around him) in.
Sex, which was created by God for the marriage bed, has such force, that God literally said it can make two people one. No, not one in terms of becoming one person, but they become one first spiritually, then emotionally, mentally and then physically.
Yes, sex is a spiritual force first. It's hard to explain, but when two people become sexually involved something spiritual happens – whether its spiritual darkness or spiritual light will depend on the two individuals involved.
Then they become emotionally and mentally combined. That's why two people who have had sexual relationship together say they find it hard to leave each other and even when they do declare that their relationship is over, they may go through a long, rough, painful process of trying to get that person out of their mind and out of their heart.
That's because they became spiritually connected as well as mentally and emotionally connected. So, people spend a long time trying to mentally get rid of someone and trying to forget someone they've had sexual relationships with, all the time not knowing that things are wrong in their spirits.
See, that's what happens when you awaken love before its time. I believe that's the crux of what Solomon was talking about when he advised his son not to awaken love before its time. Too many young people have fallen into that trap.
These days it's easier now for kids to fall into such a trap because this world is so sexually charged.
Sex is everywhere – on the television, the computer, on cell phones, in magazines, in music, even in everyday conversations. It has become so common place that it seems acceptable for kids in their teens (even younger) to become sexually involved.
But don't fall into the trap. It's a pit that will be hard to get out of and it will destroy you mentally and emotionally.
Let me point out something that I have discovered over the years – your body cannot be trusted. I know that may be hard to understand, but believe me when I say that your body will betray you. For instance, you should be aware of the fact that your body develops appetites and sometimes those appetites become so strong and so demanding, that they become a person's driving force in life.
That's why people end up with certain addictions, because their bodies have developed an appetite for a certain thing and then it becomes almost impossible to live without it. If your body becomes accustomed to eating certain foods, it develops an appetite for those foods and you may find yourself locked in a battle of the bulge, as your body craves more and more food, the kind that may not be healthy for you to consume.
Sex is the same way. When young people become involved in sex at a very young age, they begin to develop an appetite for sex that will go with them for the rest of their lives. Your first sexual experience (especially for guys) will begin you on a road that has no end, and exactly where the road leads to is uncertain.

The more sex you have, the more sex you want. It's like drug addicts who constantly chase that first initial high, but can never find it. So they use more and more drugs in hopes of getting that same feeling they had the first time they began using drugs.

Once your body becomes accustomed to sex, believe me, it's an appetite that will never go away. Of course that's not a bad thing, if you're a married person who's in love with your mate and living in a God-Covenant. But for those people who begin sexual relationships at a very young age, not even marriage can solve their sexual addictions. That's what causes infidelity and results in divorce.

The more sex you have the more your body craves sex, and if that is not put into perspective, it can become a serious addiction which can destroy you. Of course, it appears as if the problem is a mental one, but the truth is, your body dictates to your mind what it craves and if you begin to give into that craving, you're helping your body develop a habit that's going to be hard to break.

They call it an addiction.

That addiction has destroyed marriages, churches, brought down pastors and Ministers of the gospel and even brought down kings, presidents, prime ministers and rulers of countries. That's the kind of power it has.

That's why I said your body cannot be trusted.

As you grow up from your teenage years into adulthood, you will come in contact with a number of girls and women. Some you will like, some you will not like so much and there will always be those who will stir up those hormones and sexual appetites inside of you beyond what you can ever imagine.

In your mind, you're thinking if I can just have sex with that particular person, I would be satisfied. So, you go and have sex with that person and the next day, you're still not satisfied, especially if the sexual experience was not the way you had envisioned it in your mind.

So what do you do? Your body tells you that you have to do it again and "this time get it right". Of course, the second time you may do some things differently, which you had purposed in your mind you would do, but days later, you're still not satisfied and your body craves more, perhaps a new experience with someone different.

It becomes a viscous cycle that can turn deadly.

That's why what may seem so innocent as a young person, can become so detrimental in the long run. That's the importance of not awakening love (sexual intimacy) before its time.

So, when is the right time to awaken love?

There is only one rightful place – in a marriage relationship. Any time before that will place you on an emotional roller coaster.

People and the world around you may be telling you that it's okay to have sex before or outside of a marriage relationship, but they never tell you of the heartache, emotional pain and sometimes the sexually transmitted diseases people go through who follow that kind of advice. No, they never tell you about the flip side.

Think about how complicated your life is now when it is just you. Imagine what your life would be like if you suddenly became responsible for someone else – like a new born baby. No doubt, having a baby before you're ready will put a strain on you emotionally, mentally, physically and financially and it can negatively affect you when you transition into manhood. There have been many young people who thought that they were ready to become parents, but once that baby was born and reality kicked in, many of them would break down under the pressure of raising a child.

Be warned, if you make a decision to engage in sex before you're ready, be prepared for the consequences that can follow.

You will find that friendships are time tested. Real friendships take time on the part of the people involved. Some people will come in your life as a friend for a long time and there will be short term friendships. Never be disappointed when those short-term relationships reach their end. Learn to move on.

But let me warn you, friendships with girls you are really attracted to can be a serious challenge. They can cause you to lose focus and even to lose sleep. That's why I say even when you begin a friendship relationship with a girl, stay focused on where it is you want to go in life.

Love is a beautiful thing. It can make you feel as if you're on cloud nine and sometimes it can make you feel invincible. Marriage is even better, especially when you marry someone who supports you, who supports your dreams and who loves you for who you are.

Another aspect of this I would like to bring to your mind is found in the book of Proverbs, where it says "Guard your heart with all diligence, for out of it are the issues of life" (Proverbs 4:23). In other words, don't let any and everybody inside your heart.

These days, people throw around the word "Love" as if it was a "get out of jail free pass", but the truth is love may be easy to say, but sometimes, it's hard to do. That's because true love is not selfish, it's not about you.

And if you haven't noticed it by now, the world in which we live is very selfish – people are only concerned with themselves, their needs, their wants and what's gonna make them happy. People do things out of selfish motives.

Love - true Love, is the complete opposite of that.

True love is concerned about the other person and their needs.

So guard your heart against people who are quick to say they love you. True love is known by its actions.

Don't be quick to surrender your heart to the first girl who says she loves you, after only knowing you for a few days or a few weeks. Guard your heart with all diligence.

The reason the verse warns us to guard our hearts is because we live life from our hearts, and if our hearts are shattered and full of pain and hurt, that's the way we will live. There's a saying "hurting people hurt others". The more your heart gets hurt, the more pain and hurt you will live with and express towards others.

There is no pain like that of a broken heart! You will know it when you experience it.

Becoming A Man Of Your Word

Let's take another turn for a minute, to look at another step that must be considered as you prepare to leave your teenage years and move into adulthood.

To be successful as a man you must become a person of your word. How reliable you are about keeping your word will go a long way in whether or not people can rely on you.

Can you be counted on to keep your word?

Can your friends rely on something you promised them, no matter how long ago?

Are you a person of your word?

I know, as teenagers, there is the tendency to believe that life is not all that serious, so all this talk about keeping your word is really crazy. But the truth is, if you begin at an early age to learn to be true to your word, it will determine how successful you can become in business once you become a man.

Maybe you don't know this as yet, but a man is only as good as his word. No, maybe you won't understand that now, but you will hear that statement a few more times as you grow into adulthood.

Have you ever heard the popular saying "say what you mean and mean what you say".

Do you realize that children depend on people keeping their word? All kids take what their parents promise them to heart, that's why it's a problem when you promise a child that you would take him somewhere and not fulfill that promise.

A dad who may promise his son that he will be there for his birthday and who never shows up, may have a number of valid reasons why he couldn't make it, but the truth is, that child has no interest in hearing what the father has to say.

In his mind, dad never keeps his word.

That's the power of one keeping his word.

Even you as a teenager, you depend on people keeping their word, or their promise to you. And yes, you would get upset if people didn't keep their word to you.

These days, people say things out of habit, out of obligation and sometimes they say things as a plain ole lie. Sometimes people have the tendency to say something to get rid of someone whom they feel may be "bugging" them or being a nuisance. So, in order to get rid of them, they agree to something they know full well they never have any intentions of doing.

Have you ever heard someone promise faithfully that they would attend a certain party or an event and never show up? They don't bother to call, they just don't show up, and they don't see anything wrong with that.

Their excuse? "Hey, something came up," or "I got caught up doing something else and couldn't get out".

Of course, it all seems harmless, and on the surface, maybe it is, but in the long run, once people find out that your word means nothing, they will have a serious problem trusting you or believing you.

Have you ever heard about the story of the "boy who cried wolf"? It was a story about a boy who lived in a small town that was constantly invaded by vicious wolves. So much so that the town's people had developed a code word, where if anyone saw a wolf coming in the distance, they should shout out "wolf" and that would alert everyone in the town of the dangers pending. This little boy, who must have been lacking attention, decided to have some fun, so he would go in the town square of his small town and yell out "wolf" and watch as people scatter in horror. He would laugh and laugh as he watched the people running into their homes.

The boy did this on a number of occasions until the people realized that he was playing a game on them for his amusement. They chastised the boy and he went away to go play and before he knew it, he saw a wolf coming at him in the field, and so the little boy began to cry out "wolf, wolf".

But because the people in the town knew that the boy's words were unreliable or that it was just another joke, they ignored him. The wolf sprang on the little boy and devoured him.

The moral of the story? Never say anything you don't mean.

In decades gone by multi-million dollar deals were sealed with a handshake and a promise by both parties that they would each fulfill their end of the agreement. Business got done, shops were built, railroads were constructed and millions of people were employed by people being true to their word.

These days business is done much differently. Sure, they shake hands, but that's after numerous contracts have been witnessed by a room full of lawyers and signed more times than you can shake a stick at.

Yet, believe it or not, even after taking such measures, some of those deals still fall through because one party did not follow through on their agreement to carry out a part of the deal. Many court cases are based on people not fulfilling their part of the deal – or in other words, people not keeping their word.

Some business partners have been left holding the bag when a business falls apart because the other business partner did not keep his/her end of the deal.

Be assured, saying what you mean and meaning what you say is vital to your success as a person, a teenager, an employee, a businessman, a father and a husband.

In other words, become a man of integrity.

Let your word be your bond, no matter what the circumstances.

If you know you have no plans of doing something or going somewhere let the person who may be requiring you to do something or go somewhere know that you will be unable to do it. Tell them that up front.

Don't give the false impression that you will go and never show up. As far as the other person is concerned, you lied to them.

You may ask, what if I did have intentions on doing something or going somewhere and something really did come up, what do I do? Well, if it's possible, call the person right away and let them know your dilemma and see if it's something that you can do later or attend at another time.

Sure, no one's perfect and things really do come up that may be beyond your control. It's okay to let the person know that. But it's creating a habit of not keeping your word that can be a problem.

Just as I have admonished you to start to become a person of integrity, let me also warn you not to hang out with people who lack integrity. You may not be able to rely on them in a time of need.

Also, when you become a man and you get into business, never do business with people who lack integrity. If you find someone who "gives his word" for everything and never follows through on any of it, run fast through the nearest exit.

Can you imagine if your life depended on a person like that?

As a means of definition, to me integrity is when what you say lines up with what you do.

Developing integrity is not something that happens overnight. In fact, becoming a man of your word is something that starts at a young age.

Some kids feel that telling little "white lies" is harmless, but they're not. The practice of telling lies can lead to bigger transgressions. That's why it is so important to develop the habit of being honest and being a person of your word from an early age.

They say practice makes perfect, so the more you make a deliberate effort to become a man of your word, it would become second nature to you.

In fact, Proverbs 11:3 says this "The integrity of the upright shall guide them, but the willful contrariness and crookedness of the treacherous shall destroy them."

In other words, integrity can lead you in the right direction and help you make right decisions.

LIVE BY YOUR CONVICTIONS

Like a lack of integrity, living by one's convictions is something that seems to be out of style these days. Those who talk about trying to live by certain convictions (especially Biblical convictions) are usually laughed at or considered to be the odd ball.

But in decades past, people stood for what they believed and they never compromised.

When you are willing to believe in certain ideals and stand by them, you've reached a point of no return in terms of growing up.

What does it mean to stand by your convictions? It's believing certain ideals and choosing never to compromise those ideals, no matter what. It's a tough way to live and only a very strong person can carry out such a way of life.

Now, while there are so many philosophies or man-made ideals that many people live by, I want to suggest that your convictions find their roots in the Bible.

While there are many other principles and ideals from the Bible that are not specified in the Ten Commandments, I believe that those basic 10 principles which God gave to man-kind by writing it with his own fingers, are principles, if you base your life upon, will take you a long way through life (Deuteronomy 5:6-21).

Living by your convictions means that no matter where you are in this world (home or abroad) or no matter what the circumstances are that may surround you, choosing to not go against your basic core beliefs is how you will live your life.

In other words, no matter how tough things may be economically, if you stand by the conviction that it is wrong to steal, then you will not steal. Even under peer pressure, your convictions can keep you. If all your "friends" make a decision to go and harm someone or to kill someone, your conviction and belief of not killing another human being will keep you from making that kind of decision.

It's not an easy way to live, but it's possible.

Sure, there are certain consequences that can result from you living by certain convictions; you may be picked on and called names; you may be punished by the laws of the world for standing on the principles of God, or you may even lose your job or be falsely accused, but let me encourage you to never abandon your convictions.

If you make a decision to stand on the word of God and to live by his principles, He will keep you, no matter what happens.

Let me offer you a Biblical example of a young man who chose to live by his principles.

Daniel was a teenager when he was taken into captivity in Babylon (refer to Daniel 1:1-4) He was so bent on living by his convictions and the laws of his God that it was known throughout the kingdom and people respected him for that.

That's one of the benefits of living by your convictions.

People were so impressed with Daniel's way of life that when it came time for the King to appoint people to oversee his money and his administration of the kingdom, they recommended Daniel and a few others who shared the same convictions. (Daniel 6:1-2).

Another benefit of living by God's principles – promotion.

Even after getting promoted and holding one of the highest offices in the Kingdom, Daniel never lost sight of his convictions and his decision to live by the principles of God. Always remember that, promotion does not mean you abandon the principles and convictions that got you there.

Daniel was so bent on living by his convictions that those who wanted to see him destroyed realized that the only way to do that was to have his convictions go against the laws of the land (Daniel 6:4-5).

They created a law that would require Daniel abandoning his convictions and Godly principles. Suddenly, Daniel found himself in a position of having to make a tough decision; if he would abide by the new law of the land and abandon his Godly convictions, he would get to keep his big time position, which no doubt was paying him well.

If he would chose to stand by his convictions he would risk losing everything that he had worked so hard to achieve.

Daniel chose to stand by his convictions. He realized that promotion comes from God and therefore chose not to go against God and his word.

Of course the decision to stick by his convictions (Daniel 6:10) caused him to lose his job and to even be thrown into the Lion's Den, which at the time was like being sentenced to death in the electric chair or by lethal injection.

That's the consequences of living by your convictions.

Daniel chose to die than to abandon his Godly convictions. That was no easy decision to make. But if you read the entire story God honored his decision to live by His principles and delivered Daniel from death.

Living by your convictions can help you through your tough teenage years when peer pressure constantly weighs on you. It can help you through those free-wheeling, yet hard times of college life, when you will have to daily make decisions to live by the principles of God. Choosing to live by Godly convictions will help you on your job and even help you in running a business.

WHAT DOES YOUR CHARACTER SAY ABOUT YOU?

If you are a sports fan, no doubt you have seen the television news or read in the papers about ball players who sign mega million dollar deals to play a sport they love. It's amazing how much money these guys get paid. I'm talking about guys signing a deal for one year to play ball and make like five million dollars. And that's on the low side.

Imagine that, $5 million in one year, just to play either baseball, football, basketball, or some other sport, and depending on the sport, some contracts can be even bigger. I've read of basketball players signing six-year contracts for up to $60 million. You know how long the majority of people would have to work to even get close to sixty million dollars?

I don't care how many letters one may have behind his name, or how many degrees a person may have making, $60 million dollars is something not even a scientist can make in that period of time.

That's why so many young people dream about playing in the NBA, the NFL, MLB, NHL or some other professional sport. Sports is a very lucrative business and it produce millions on a yearly basis.

What is so amazing is to read about these guys signing these kinds of contracts, hear about the kinds of houses they live, the amount of cars they have, and yet a few months later read about these same guys losing it all because of some dumb fight in a club or for driving under the influence or for domestic abuse.

You have to ask yourself, how can a guy who make so much money make such dumb choices? How is that possible?

Bad choices, poor decisions.

You see, they are perfect examples of guys who have great talent, but no character. Their talent took them some place where they had no character to keep them. You see, money don't make you a better person, it only magnifies who you already are. Remember the saying "more money makes you more of who you already are"?

Character is missing.

Back to the ball players for a minute, I've even seen these guys with huge contracts get into an argument on the field or on the court, which eventually turns into a brawl. They get suspended and fined millions of dollars and eventually have to publicly offer an apology.

I always wondered what in the world can someone say to me that would make me get so angry and forget that I get paid millions of dollars in one year just to play a sport. If I'm getting $60 million in six years, there isn't anything in the world anyone can say to me to get me angry enough to fight them on the ball field.

Whatever they say, all I would do is just think about my $60 million dollar contract. At the end of the day, I do my job, I get paid.

Of course, it's easy to say that until you find yourself in that actual situation.

Don't get me wrong, not all of these guys who play sports are like that. Some of them who come from good homes (even some who might not have come from stable homes) have good principles and go far in their respective sport and they even invest and use their money wisely, being careful to avoid the bad behavior or the media hype.

But those are the guys who had good character even before they signed their name on the dotted line for $60 million.

But anyone who has grown up in a hostile environment and all he/she knows is violence, they will respond in violence when their back is against the wall or when they feel threatened. That's the law of human nature. It's the law of character.

The kind of environment we grow up in will determine the kind of character we develop. You see, character is really who you are when no one's looking. It's the real you. You build good character by what you believe in and the way you think about the world around you. What you think affects what you believe and what you believe determines how you act and react to people and situations around you.

Your goal is to develop a Godly character and become a man of substance. You do that by reading and living by God's word. Kids who are taught to respect other people and other people's things will act that way even when they're out of their parent's presence. That's character.

Good character is not something that can be faked. Yes, people can pretend to be nice for a while, but eventually the real them becomes exposed. There's an old saying that a wolf may disguise itself in sheep's clothing to get among the fold, but eventually the wolf within that sheep clothing will expose itself.

There's also another story I heard about a snake that wanted to get across a river, but was afraid to get in the water. A huge bird came along and landed on the bank of the river near the snake. The two got to talking and eventually the snake told the bird of his dilemma. The bird offered the snake a ride on its back so that he could fly him across the river, but on one condition, that the snake does not harm him.

So they took off, but as soon as the bird got into the air, the snake started to wrap itself around the bird's body and began to squeeze. The bird was able to hold on until they landed safely on the other side. When the snake got off, the bird asked the snake why did he do that, considering they had a deal that he would not hurt him.

The snake said "I couldn't help it, that's just my nature. It's who I am."

You see, the snake was only acting in character, which was to squeeze the life out of anything that came its way. It was his nature.

People normally confuse personality with character, but there is a difference.

A personality is something that can be turned off and on. Of course some people have good personalities and some people have bad personalities, but a person with a normally bad personality can put on a good personality for a period of time.

Do you know of guys who curse after every other word, but who can control that and not say one curse word when they're around a priest or a pastor, or around someone they respect? However, the minute they get from around that person, they go back to cursing. They changed their personality, even if it was only for a short time.

To have a good character you will have to develop a good character.

A Little Respect Goes
A Long Way

Another step that will help you ease into the phase of manhood successfully is that of being a person who shows respect.

By now, you're probably wondering where this book is headed. It started off great, but now all this talk about being a person of your word and now talk about respect is not something you signed on for when you decided to read this book.

But stick with me for a minute and we can get through this without a scratch.

Like being a man of your word, showing respect will take you a long way into your manhood. Actually showing respect will result in people respecting you.

When I was being taught about manners and respect, I got tired of hearing about it. It took me some time to get it though, particularly during those teenage years where I felt like I knew everything there was to know about life and the world around me.

It wasn't until I was out there on my own, began working on a job and had to be more interactive with so many different kinds of people that I finally got a handle on what others were trying to tell me all of those years.

Back then, respect was something that was held up as sacred. It was not a "do it if you please" sort of standard, it was a "do it or else" standard.

It was not a matter of if I would show people respect, it was a matter of how many times in one day would I have to show respect. And when I was growing up, that meant many times in one day.

We said "Good morning" and "Good afternoon" to total strangers. Everyone older than you was referred to as "Yes sir" or "Yes ma'am", "no sir" or "no ma'am". It was the order of the day. And failure to show such respect could result in discipline, first by the person to whom you showed disrespect, then by your parents when they were told why you had gotten punished in the first place.

But how things have changed.

Today, respect has become a "bad" word and many people don't see the need in being courteous or showing respect to anyone. As a teenager, showing respect always seems like a challenge, perhaps because many young people were not taught the value of respect, nor was it ever demanded of them.

Too many teenagers and young adults feel that showing respect to someone who is older or to someone who holds a certain position or office is really something that is "Old fashioned".

Why such a big deal about having respect?

It's a characteristic that reflects insight into one's up-bringing. You can tell a lot about a person by the way they respect or disrespect people around them.

When parents refuse to teach their children to respect others and how to respect other people's property, a societal decline becomes inevitable.

Having respect for others teaches you how to respect someone else's space. Have you ever put down your ipod or something and went to check on something and when you came back someone else had it in their hands, playing with it?

How did that make you feel? Even if it's someone you knew, the fact that they did not even bother to ask you to use it made you feel upset and angry. You may not admit it, but in your mind, that's being very disrespectful of other people's things.

That's how other people feel when you show them disrespect.

You respect other people's property and things by not removing or taking anything that belongs to someone else without first getting their permission. If something does not belong to you, leave it alone. If there is a fruit tree in someone else's yard and you would like to have some fruit, you don't take it upon yourself to just go into that person's yard and go into their tree and take what you want. The respectful thing to do would be to go and knock on the person's door and ask if you may be allowed to get some of their fruit.

If they give you permission, go ahead and get some fruit and ask the owner if they would like for you to pick some for them as well. When you're done say "thank you" and leave.

If the owner says "no, you cannot go into the tree", then tell them "thank you" and leave their property. Anything other than that is called stealing.

This may seem like a trivial matter, but you would be surprised at how many arguments, fights and even deaths have occurred from a simple thing as not having respect for other people's property.

It's disturbing to see how many young people speak to and treat older people. They don't open doors for their senior citizens, they push right by them in stores, sometimes knocking them over and some young people use profane language in the presence of older people.

All of that is considered to be disrespectful.

To me raising a child who shows disrespect is setting the environment for a breeding ground of criminality, because that child is raised to believe that that he can do what he wants, when he wants, without any dire consequences.

We all know that not to be true. In fact, society operates on certain laws and if those laws are broken, it will result in certain consequences. Not even society appreciates any of its laws being disrespected.

The Bible has a lot to say about respect, which only goes to show that even God takes respect serious.

In the book of Leviticus 19:3, God, in talking to Moses warns the Israelites "each of you must respect his mother and father and you must observe my Sabbaths. I am the Lord."

In the Book of 1 Timothy, the apostle Paul said that Deacons and their wives are to be treated with respect and honor. In 1 Peter 2:17 the apostle Paul again stressed that we are to "show proper respect to everyone; love the brotherhood of believers, fear God, honor the King."

The Bible says "Bring up a child in the way he should go and when he is old he will not depart from it."

My mother was right when she said that respect and manners will take you around the world. Once you learn the art of respect, it will take you places you could only dream of. I know that sounds far-fetched, but it's true.

Show respect for people who are older than you, no matter where you go. It does not matter if they're related to you or not. If you step into a room, always say "good morning" or "good afternoon" if there are people there in the room.

Always say "excuse me" when trying to get around someone or when interrupting a conversation. When asked a question, your answer should always be "yes sir" or "no sir". If you did not hear what was said or did not understand what was said always say "pardon me?"

You must show respect for your teachers and those placed in authority over you. You must always show respect to your employer or your supervisor and you must always have respect for the laws of the land and for those authority figures who enforce such laws.

Disrespectful adults usually raise disrespectful kids; disrespectful kids turn into disrespectful adults, which leads to a society of disrespectful people. If that's allowed to spread, imagine what the world would be like.

Never, ever hang out or befriend kids who show no respect for their parents, for adults or for the laws of the land. Those kids are bad news and will only lead you in the wrong direction. Their show of disrespect is an indicator that they will eventually find themselves in some sort of trouble.

The Apostle Paul in the book of 1 Corinthians 15:33 says "Bad company corrupts good morals." In other words if you continuously hang out with kids who have no respect for others, they will eventually influence you in that way.

Begin to show respect at home for your parents and even for your siblings. This is the foundation for a life of respect and manners.

Honor your mother and father

It's a task to try and use the words "honor your mother and father" to teenagers, because many teenagers find that hard to do. In fact to tell a child today the value of honoring his parents, that child will look at you as if you are out of your mind.

"What do you mean honor my parents?" is the question he would ask, with a serious look of confusion on his face. "My father is an idiot who is never around and my mother is crazy," he quickly adds, as a means of justifying his disrespect for his parents.

Kids today have become so accustomed to disrespecting their parents that it's become the cool thing to do. They talk to their parents anyway they feel like and they find some of the meanest things they can think of to tell the women who carried them for nine months and went through pain to deliver them.

I've heard little kids curse at their parents, without any sense of remorse or fear. What it must feel like when a four year old child who can't have his way kicks off into a tantrum and shouts out at his mother "I hate you!"

Some mothers have said it feels like a knife going straight through the heart. Others said that a knife in the heart would be less painful than what it really feels like to hear a child tell them something like that.

Here in the Western culture we have descended far into a pit of disrespect for parents. The truth is, children not honoring their parents may be the reason for such a high level of criminal activity, gang violence, failure among baby-boomers and even poverty.

The Bible warns us to "honor your mother and father so that your days may be long upon the earth." (Exodus 20"12).

God was so serious about this that it is repeated throughout the Bible, from the old testament through to the new testament. It could be found in Exodus 20:12, Deut. 5:16, Matthew 15:4, Matthew 19:19 and Eph. 6:2.

Children may find all sorts of reasons why they don't feel they should honor their parents. Perhaps their parents are abusive, disrespectful to them, a drunk, a prostitute, or just plain mean to them as kids.

And the truth is there are parents who have been some or all of those things towards their kids and it's hurtful to see parents abuse kids.

However, the Bible tells us to honor our parents, even if we don't like them or like the things they do. It doesn't say honor your mother and father IF….it just tells children to honor their mother and father.

Yes, I feel that respect is something that is earned and is a two-way street, but honor is not the same thing as respect. Honor is not earned, it is something that comes with one's position. Just like God tells us to honor the King (President, Prime Minister or Premier, depending on where you live), it's not so much about honoring the person as it is about honoring the office which that person holds.

You may not like the president of the United States, but you must honor the office of the President.

The same thing applies with our parents. Some parents may not be worthy of any respect by the way they treat their kids and others, but God still warns children to honor the office of the mother and father. Some parents have been and are extremely mean to their children, even to the point of abusing them, so I can see why children find it hard to honor parents like that.

There are some parents who have even abandoned their children on the streets, leaving them to fend for themselves; some have even given their children over into prostitution to make money for them and in certain parts of the world mothers and fathers are selling their children into slavery just for money.

How can you honor parents like that? It's hard and to the natural mind not only impossible, but crazy to even try to do so.

The truth is, only God can give a child the kind of love and grace to honor parents like that. To try to do so by human standard and human strength would only end in pain and hurt. Yet, the Bible calls on children to honor their parents.

You honor them by acknowledging that they are your parents (whether you like that fact or not) and you answer them with respect, even if you don't think they deserve it. Like I said, for those kids raised by abusive parents, only God can give them that kind of love to even begin to honor their parents.

However, there are kids who are not abused, who, in fact live on the other side of the balance, where they are given everything they could need and want, yet, they still refuse to honor their parents.

Honoring one's parents (especially for those kids with abusive or mean parents) may be a difficult thing to do, but God call on kids to do it, not for the parents' sake, but really for the sake of the child. It says "…so that it may go well with you and that your days may be long upon the earth."

There is the key to long life and having a good life.

Who ever thought the key would be in honoring one's mother and father? I always thought success was based on one's gifts and talents; on one's ability to talk their way to the top or based on who you know and their willingness to help you get to the top.

No, the Bible says success in life is based on a child honoring his mother and father.

That explains why today we see so many kids walking the streets, strung out on drugs, going crazy in their minds or living in sickness and poverty. That explains why kids are dying at such a young age – all because of a lack of honor for their mother and father.

Some kids have led hard, tough lives because of a lack of respect for their parents, and the sad part is, they never associate their lack of honor for their parents, with their hard times in life. But the two go hand-in-hand.

God made a promise that if children honor their parents it will go well with them and they would live a long life.

The Japanese have mastered the art of honoring their parents. In fact the Japanese are so bent on honoring their parents that they even honor their ancestors who may have died decades ago. They are encouraged to not only honor their parents, but to honor their grandparents and the parents before, as well as to honor their culture.

Perhaps the Japanese have stumbled onto something which we here in the Western Culture have missed and that is the secret to honoring our parents.

Everyone Pays A Price For The Decisions They Make

Choices, choices, choices. Decisions, decisions, decisions – those are the majority of the things that you will have to do each and every day. Even when you're not consciously making a choice, you are. Even when you're not choosing to decide, in some way you have made a decision.

There was a time when teenagers didn't have so many choices available to them and so it kind of made the choices they did have before them much easier. Today, there are so many more decisions and choices facing today's teenagers that it can be mind boggling.

The thing about choices is that for every action there is an opposite reaction. For every choice, there is a consequence and for every decision we make there is a price to pay – whether good or bad.

That's the way life has been designed.

Every consequence is preceded by a decision and a choice. Look at the way the universe is set up, a plant has to die for seed to be planted, every time we breathe in, we eventually have to breathe out. Life is us breathing in and death is us breathing out.

On any given weekend there is a wedding and a funeral taking place at the same time. On one hand there is joyous celebration and on the next, there is mourning and grief. That's the way life is.

So, since every decision we make is followed by a consequence, you have to be careful to try and make as many good decisions you can during the course of your life. Of course, no one's perfect, but if you learn at an early age that every choice you make today will help shape your tomorrow, it should encourage you to always be aware of the kinds of decisions you are making in your life.

A decision not to go to school will result in a lack of education, which will mean a tough life ahead in terms of finding employment, making money and living a good life; a decision to hang out with the wrong crowd could affect how you view the world around you and as a result it will affect how you respond to that world around you; a decision to disobey the laws of the land could result in you losing your freedom and rights as a citizen of the land once you go to prison; a decision to live a promiscuous life could result in heartache and possibly contracting a sexually transmitted disease.

Every decision to save money today could mean a life of prosperity and having more than you need to live on in the future. On the other hand, a decision to spend every dime that comes into your hands today will result in poverty and lack in the future.

Yes, life is all about making decisions and making the right choices.

And each decision, each choice comes with a price tag, some more costly than others. One of the biggest mistakes you could ever make is to assume that your choices and your decisions for today will only have an effect on today.

No, the way you're living today is basically based on the choices you made yesterday and tomorrow's condition of your life will be based on the decisions and choices you make today. God Almighty has given us as human beings a free will and the ability to choose. He gives us the information we need, but leaves the final decision up to us. In Deuteronomy 30:19 The Lord (through Moses) told the Children of Israel to make a choice – "This day I call Heaven and earth as witnesses against you, that I have set before you life and death, blessings and curses. Now choose life, so that you and your children may live and that you may love the Lord your God, listen to his voice and hold fast to him."

Also don't fall into the trap of thinking that the choices that you make will only affect you. The truth is in one way or the other all of us are connected to someone and the choices we perceive to be personal choices will eventually have an effect on someone else. We never sin in isolation.

When the first man Adam and his wife Eve made a choice to eat the forbidden fruit, there was no one else around at the time, but because all of mankind was somehow inside of them, their decision affected every man and woman that came after them.

Our choices will determine what kind of price we pay for our decisions.

Choosing to just hang out and waste time, will affect the kind of future you will create. That's a high price to pay in the long run. A decision to use your time wisely will affect how you live the rest of your life in the future. The choice may seem like a high price at the time, but in the long run that kind of choice will pay off in dividends.

It's amazing that when you're young and full of life, there seems to be so much time ahead of you. As a teenager, you figure the ages 25 and up seem like a long way ahead, but time moves so quickly that before you know it, you're celebrating your 30th birthday and you're wondering where the time went.

It bothers me when I walk pass a group of teenagers and I hear them complaining about having nothing to do and about how bored they are, despite the fact that they're standing around, or hanging out wasting time.

That's why I encourage you, even as a youngster and a teenager never consider time as something to be wasted. Sure, you should have fun, but never spend your prime years just having fun, partying or just hanging out. Use those years to improve yourself, improve your gifts and talents and learn all you can about the world in which you live.

It's amazing that there are so many things you can learn and you will never run out of something new to learn no matter how long you live. The world is much bigger than it appears, life more challenging than it seems and people are more complicated than you can ever imagine. So you see, learning is a never ending cycle.

Make up your mind now to pay the price of discipline and commitment so that you may reap the rewards in the future. Yes, there may be one or two parties you may have to miss, but trust me, there is always a party somewhere, sometime.

So, maybe you will miss a few because of your commitment to improve yourself, but put in the time, do the work, obtain the degree, land a great career and you can throw your own parties later on.

I'm not suggesting that you become a book worm, what some consider to be "a nerd" or some recluse who never goes anywhere or who never have any fun. On the contrary, life is to be enjoyed and you should have fun, but always remember that if all you do is play now, once you get into your future you may find that many of your playmates have moved on and you're left standing alone holding a party favor, with no one around to help you celebrate.

No, have fun and live life, but live life in balance. Remember balance is one of the keys of life. Enjoy your share of life while sticking to your standards, discipline and commitment to improve your life.

This is something you will have to practice even more once you begin college. With no one there to make you do your studies and attend classes, you will have to become a man of discipline. You will have to know when to say "no" to certain things in order to complete your class assignments.

These are grown up decisions you will have to make, but learning to make such decisions will be easier if you begin to learn to make right choices now as a teenager.

A number of years ago, there were some television ads on mostly urban and African American stations encouraging young people who were not in college to attend some community college or do some courses over the internet. In the ads one of the spokespersons would always say "time's gonna pass anyway, so why not let it pass with you doing something for you."
I like that.
Yes, time will pass whether you waste time or use it constructively. So why not let it pass with you doing something to make yourself better?
Proverbs 19:15 says this "Laziness brings on deep sleep and the shiftless man goes hungry."
No, making right choices will not be easy, considering you live in a world that's so negative and competitive at the same time. But you're also living in a world where for the most part, everyone is looking out for themselves. The truth is, people outside of your family and close friends may care about you based on what you can do for them.
Beyond that, everyone looks out for number one. But if you remember that every choice you make now will affect your future, it should steer you into making choices that are positive and Godly.
Many people don't like the price they have to pay for the decisions they've made in their lives. I've heard people cry and moan about how their lives turned out by the time they reached a certain age. Many people have been there and done that, but you can avoid getting there if you realize that you have the power to make the right decisions.
Let me point out another nugget of truth I want you to receive – if at all possible try to avoid destructive habits.
What do I mean?
There are certain vices in life that can develop into destructive habits. In the chapter about sex, I talked about how promiscuity can become a destructive habit, simply because if it is allowed to go unchecked, it will end up controlling you, which could lead to you making bad decisions and stupid choices.
There are also the vices of alcohol abuse, getting involved in drugs or being consumed with gambling.
Famous musicians, talented actors and athletes, millionaires and preachers have all fallen victim to one or more of these vices. When asked why they fell so far, many had no reasons why and felt that it was just their lot in life. But the truth is they fell victim to one of those vices.
That's why they're called destructive habits.
Because they are habits, that means they have to develop over a period of time, and they're developed through a series of choices and decisions. Every decision made to give in to either one of those vices takes you on the road that leads closer to becoming a destructive habit.
If you find that you may have some tendency towards one or more of these vices, remember, that the more times you give in, the easier it will become the next time, and the next time. Every choice to give in to that vice makes it easier for you to develop the habit. That's one of those things you have to nip in the bud and don't allow it to spring up, or it will destroy you.
Some of these habits are done for social acceptance; like drinking socially or making bets for the fun of it. They may all seem innocent at first glance, and that's the trap.
Proverbs 1:29 says "Since they hated knowledge and did not choose to fear the Lord, since they would not accept my advice and spurned my rebuke, they will eat the fruit of their ways and be filled with the fruit of their scheme."
It's called paying the price for your decisions.
Talk to someone who's in prison or who has been in prison and perhaps he will tell you how he wished he could take back what he did or how he wished he could turn back the hands of time so that he could make a different decision at the time of that incident that landed him in jail.

But the truth is we cannot turn back the hands of time. We cannot take back what we've said or what we've done. We must reap the consequences of our decisions, whether good or bad. Proverbs 3:1-4 is my plea for you "My Son, do not forget my teaching, but keep my commands in your heart, for they will prolong your life many years and bring you prosperity. Let love and faithfulness never leave you; bind them around your neck, write them on the tablet of your heart. Then you will win favor and a good name in the sight of God and man."

Don't Be Afraid To Dream Big

One of the beauty about youth is the fact that you're free to dream.
When you're young, you have the freedom to dream, and not just dream, but you can dare to dream big. You see, when you reach a certain age, only certain dreams are allowed to be entertained by your mind.
As hard as it is to admit sometimes, the truth is, some dreams are for certain times in our lives. Don't get me wrong, with God, all things are possible, however, when it comes to dreams there are certain things that play a big role – like our age, our accessibility to resources and our responsibilities. There are certain dreams that are just for the young, and then there are dreams that can happen at any age.
With youth on your side, never be afraid of dreaming big. As a teenager, no dream is impossible, as long as you are willing to work hard to make that dream come true. The good thing with having age on your side is the fact that, with all things being equal, you just may have time on your side.
Of course, that is not always the case, because we have seen the stories where young people are dying faster than older people. That's because the lifestyle choices of most young people today places them at risk for dying early.
However, as long as you make right choices and avoid addictive behavior, you can extend the time you have of making your dreams become a reality.
So, now that you know you are free to dream big, what is your dream?
On November 4, 2008, Barack Obama became the first Afro-American to take over as president of the United States of America. He became the United States' 44th President.
It was more than just history being made, for many black Americans (and blacks in the Western Hemisphere) it was a dream come true. Over 40 years before, some blacks were unable to even vote in an election, but 40 years later, not only were blacks allowed to vote, but a black person became president, something many said would never happen in America.
But his election as president proves one thing – nothing is impossible!
That's why I encourage you to never be afraid of dreaming big. Never think something is too big or impossible for you to accomplish. Never limit yourself and never allow others to limit you. I once heard someone say that we are only limited by our own thoughts and our own minds. If we think we can, then we can; if we think we can't, then we won't.

Having dreams is essential not just to being successful, but dreams are what motivates people. They help give us hope that we can be better people and live a better life. Dreams also give us purpose in life. Nothing can be worse than living a life without a sense of purpose.

I've seen people with what I would describe as having great jobs, successful careers, acquiring substantial assets, living in beautiful homes and driving state-of-the-art automobiles, yet they find themselves unhappy.

Have you ever wondered how that could be, because when you think about it, to have all of those things should make anyone happy. While the reasons for those individuals' state of unhappiness varies, one of the most prevalent reason is a sense of feeling unfulfilled.

Some people can accomplish many things, but if they're not doing something they love or something they feel they were born to do, they just go through the motions and although they may acquire much wealth and fame, their need for a sense of purpose had not been met.

Remember, your dreams will normally fall in line with your purpose in life. In other words, that dream you have that burns inside of you, eager to be exposed, is normally tied to what it is God has put you on this earth to do.

It's your assignment.

Especially when you find yourself thinking about it day and night and in your mind, you can see yourself doing whatever the dream may be. In your mind, you're already living it. For the most part, that's a dream that's been placed in your heart by God and it's burning on the inside of you because he's nudging you to go ahead and bring that dream to past.

Some people dream about doing things they may have seen someone else do and that's fine, except, if it's not a part of their purpose in life, they may not have that kind of passion for that thing. Sometimes people want to do something someone else is doing because they see that it brings great financial rewards. But as I said earlier, making all of the money in the world, without living out your own dream will leave you feeling empty and unfulfilled.

The Bible says, "Many are the plans in a man's heart, but it's the Lord's purpose that will be established. (Proverbs 19:21).

Yes, people live other people's dreams and that too leaves them feeling unfulfilled and unhappy. Children try to live up to their parent's expectations and follow a career path they feel their parents would want them to follow.

Some parents try to live vicariously through their children and push them to be or do something those kids may not want to do or be. I've known parents who once dreamed of being a dancer, a singer, a doctor, a speaker or even a preacher, but due to circumstances in their lives were unable to fulfill those dreams, so they push their kids to become those things they never got a chance to be.

That's why you must have your own dreams. Follow the dreams that God has placed in your heart. Why? Because the dreams that God places in your heart are specifically designed for you; for your personality and your character.

Your gifts and talents normally line up with your dreams for your life. For instance, if you have a nice voice, your dream would normally be to accomplish something along the lines of singing and performing. If you are a gifted speaker, your dreams would follow those lines of standing in front of people and speaking, maybe as a motivational speaker, a politician or even a teacher.

In other words, your talents and sometimes your personality combine efforts to create in you a dream and a purpose to fulfill.

Of course, such deductions are not written in stone and may not follow such a clear cut path. There are exceptions to every rule and sometimes your dreams may include a combination of gifts and talents and may not always end up in an obvious conclusion.

There are people who are doing things they never dreamed they would be doing. They did not have the natural propensity towards that particular thing, nor did they study it or had any plans to do it. But God knows what it is he has called each of us to do and he will give the wisdom and the courage to do what he calls us to do.

That's why it's important not to limit yourself, or to live your life in a box.

Life is much bigger than any box you may find yourself in. The possibilities in life are limitless, as long as you're willing to put in the time, have the discipline and pay the price. Having big dreams will make your life more fulfilled and richer, but let me encourage you to go after your smaller dreams first. The reason for that is when you achieve a small dream, it gives you a sense of what it feels like to have a dream come true.

Always have smaller goals to move you towards your bigger goal. The small dreams give you more confidence and accomplishing them builds your faith, which you will need to accomplish your big dreams.

You don't have to wait until you find your career path or wait until you reach 20 or 30 years of age to begin dreaming. No, dream big even while you're just a teenager. The world is a big place and there are opportunities to fulfill every dream.

That's why you should never be afraid to dream and never let your dreams die. Pursue them while you're young and you have less to lose. While you're young, you have more courage, more energy, more determination and less fear. While you're young, you still have a chance to start again if you fail the first time. That's one of the advantages of youth – time is still on your side.

But when you wait too long to attempt to accomplish your dreams, you may find it difficult to pursue those dreams because of fear.

Don't let people limit you, don't let circumstances frighten you and don't let obstacles discourage you, and never, ever give up on your dreams.

You should be aggressive when it comes to business and be aggressive when it comes to pursuing your dreams. Never sit back and wait for someone to bring your dreams to you, go out and grab them!

Don't spend all of your time watching other people live their dreams, while yours slip away. It amazes me how people can sit for hours and watch television, then go to bed, get up and go to a job they hate because it's not taking them anywhere, go home watch television and then go to bed and repeat the cycle over again the next day.

They spent all of their free time watching other people live out their dreams, while theirs go down the drain.

Knock on every door, look under every rock, part every bush, seek out every bit of information pertaining to your dream. Never let a day go by without doing something to move you closer towards your dream. Never allow yourself to become idle.

Realize that every day you live there are people out there in the world living their dreams. Somewhere in the world people are writing books, recording music, starring in movies, building skyscrapers, getting a promotion, saving lives, studying to become a doctor or a lawyer, etc., and living a better life.

Dream of living a better life. Dream of helping to make life better for others around you. Dream big. If God is inside of you, He will give you dreams that are beyond you. He's that's the kind of God. After all, he had a dream when he created the world, didn't he? Look around you, you're in the world right?

Always dream big.

Live Your Life In Balance

There is one secret in life that you must master in order to be successful and in order to get through those rough teenage years – that is learning to live life in balance.

Living life by extremes can be harmful in the long run. I know this may sound contradictory to all that I've been telling you throughout this book, but the truth is, all that I've been trying to teach you results in living a life of balance.

Yes, even though I believe that you should strive to be as rich as you can, you must also learn to be satisfied with where you are in your life (no matter which season of life you may be in); although I believe that a man must be strong, not just physically, but mentally and emotionally, a man must also know how to be tender towards those he loves and compassionate to the less fortunate; although I warned against living a life of fun and partying, you must also learn that sometimes you will have to look up from the books and enjoy your life, even if it's for a moment.

Yes, life is all about balance.

The Bible says that God approves a just scale (or a just balance), it also warns us to avoid extremes in life (Ecclesiastes 7:18).

Even God knows how important it is to live life in balance.

Ecclesiastes 3:1-8 tells us that there is a time for everything: "There is a time for everything and a season for every activity under Heaven; a time to be born and a time to die; a time to plant and a time to uproot; a time to kill and a time to heal; a time to tear down and a time to build; a time to weep and a time to laugh; a time to mourn and a time to dance; a time to scatter stones and a time to gather them; a time to embrace and a time to refrain; a time to search and a time to give up; a time to keep and a time to throw away; a time to tear and a time to mend; a time to be silent and a time to speak; a time to love and a time to hate; a time for war and a time for peace."

The inability to find a balance in life has been the downfall of many. There are those who embarked on a life to study and work hard to build a career and it has taken them all their lives to achieve it. However, by the time they look up and want to enjoy life, life has passed them by and they realize that they've been so busy that they did not have time to even pursue relationships.

In many cases these people end up living life alone. They had no time for a family life because they were always too busy in school and pursuing their career. They end up with no mate, no children and very little friends – why? Because building friendships and relationships take time, and that was the one thing they did not have.

On the other hand there are those who live their whole lives loosely and not committed to anything. They pursue no goals, do very little studying and end up without a career. They live life as it comes and have decided to live life spontaneously, not making any plans.

They too end up alone, because eventually all of their party friends leave and move on to the next "big thing" that comes along. They end up losing their relationships because they have no commitment, no discipline, no goals and no plans for life.

Those are the two basic pictures of life without balance; each one represents an extreme in life. Notice that the end result is that both end up alone. A life of balance would avoid that.

When it comes to health and religion, people do the same thing, go from one extreme to the next. There are those who are health fanatics and they exercise every single day of their lives and eat as healthy as they can every single day of their lives. They have a desire to maintain a body fat percentage of two percent and they push themselves until their body breaks down. On the extreme side of that are those who don't take care of themselves at all; they don't exercise, they eat nothing healthy; in fact the closest they come to eating vegetables is French fries and they forget that their body is like a machine and without any kind of maintenance, it will eventually break down.

Solomon hit the nail on the head again when he said "A man who fears God will avoid all extremes (Ecc. 7:18).

Balance is knowing when to laugh and when to cry; when to play and when to work, when to dance and when to keep still, knowing when to party and when to study, knowing when to say no and when to say yes; its knowing when to be tender and when to be tough.

It may seem like a hard lesson to learn, but once you learn to avoid all extremes, eventually you will strike a balance in your life.

One way to begin to learn to live life in balance is to set certain boundaries for your life.

When I was a kid, we had this thing where if there was an argument between two people, one of the persons in the argument would draw a line on the ground and dare the other person to cross it. If the other person was brave enough to cross that line, it was on and you could be sure that a fight was on the horizon.

Those were the rules of the game. That was the consequence of crossing the line.

Even today, there is a saying "you've crossed the line" when someone does or says something inappropriate or out of line.

That's the idea behind setting boundaries. There should be certain lines in your life which you, nor anyone else should not be allowed to cross. For example, if you've set up a boundary in your life on smoking or taking drugs, when someone offers it to you, you will know that that will be crossing the line and crossing your boundaries.

Once you realize that, you know that proceeding with that activity will only lead to a bad outcome.

Boundaries help keep us in balanced. They give us a sense of direction and helps making some of life's "hard" decisions and choices much easier.

All work and no play makes Jack a dull boy

Before you get the impression that I am instructing you to spend your life studying, working and developing your character, let me point out the other side of it all – play time.
Yes, play time!
Solomon says that there is a time for everything under the sun and play time is one of those times. There was an old cliché that says "All work and no play, makes Jack a dull boy." In other words, you are not complete unless you know how to play, laugh and enjoy yourself.
Playtime means so many things to so many different people; it all depends on one's personality. You might enjoy video games, watching movies, listening to your ipod, chatting on your cell phone, racing remote control cars and planes, playing some sort of sport, or even just hanging with your friends.
It's important to unwind and relax at times. You must take time out of your life to enjoy life, because you would want to avoid all extremes, you must take time to look up from the books, take a break from your work (its called vacation) and get away and have good, clean fun.
Yes, good, clean fun is still possible these days.

While on this topic of play time, I want to encourage you to involve some sort of exercise program into your play time. You see I'm convinced that exercise is a part of the whole development of a man. It strengthens the body and the mind and it gives you the energy to pursue your career, to study effectively and to be a better person.

A healthy body and a sound mind is a great combination.

I've seen so many men get so caught up in their careers that they ignore the need to exercise. As a result, their career flourishes, but eventually they have to take time from that career to recover from some sort of illness that could have perhaps been prevented through regular exercise.

Exercise keeps the body healthy and serves as a tune up for the body. Make exercise a regular part of your daily routine at an early age. Once exercise becomes a part of your lifestyle, it will be hard to break. It will also help you live longer, with all things being equal.

Of course exercise can become addictive as well and some people go overboard with it. Avoid that happening by taking a balanced approach. A commitment to exercise at least three times a week is sufficient to give you the level of tune up your body needs.

Remember, life is about balance.

So, work hard, play hard, have fun, exercise, eat healthy, pig out once in a while, live your life in balance.

Be Skillful With Your Hands

One of the Hallmarks of a man is being able to fix things.

Men were seen as the handymen around the home and everyone called on them when something was loose or a cupboard door fell off, or the bathroom sink was clogged up – everyone called on "Mr. Fix It" of the house.

Some of these guys live up to the name and they're able to fix just about anything. Some guys – well, they may have been able to fix one or two things, but for the most part, they just did not cut it as handymen.

As long as you're able to become skilled with your hands, you would never regret it a day in your life.

There used to be a point in time when boys were fascinated by men who could fix things. A boy's eyes would widen with excitement as he watched a carpenter create something special out of wood or watched a mechanic make a car roar with power.

Boys who had an opportunity to work on a construction site felt proud to be able to be a part of a group of people who constructed an entire building from the foundation to completion. Along the way, that boy would learn so many things about construction that just being able to acquire such knowledge was pay enough.

Why? Because when that boy grew into a man, he had knowledge and a skill that could not be taken from him and one that would eventually bring financial reward for him.

Today, while everyone is excited about computers, technology and communications, there are still those skills which I think every boy should learn a little about. Time has proven that even in the midst of the advancement of modern technology, people are still constructing homes, cars are still being put together on the assembly line and there are still pipes running through every bathroom inside a home.

That means all of these skills are still necessary in today's modern world, and let me encourage you to try and learn as much as you can about these various skills. Yes, I know that computers are a major part of the cars being built today and contractors use computers to design homes for them.

However, when it comes down to actually doing the work, it's still a human endeavor. So, while you advance your knowledge in the world of computers, take a little time to learn about the various skills which men continue to perform.

Have you ever been around when your parents made the decision to do some renovations on the house?

One of the frustrating aspects of such a renovation process may have been trying to find honest, reliable, capable carpenters, tile layers, electricians and builders to do the things that were needed to get the work done.

There may have been those workers who were really skilful, but they may not have really been honest and upfront; the ones who were reliable were not as skilful. As a silent witness to the frustration of this process, I'm sure you heard your parents rant and rave about the outrageous prices for labor which these people were charging to do the work.

Now consider this fact that you, yes you, can learn these skills and when the time comes for you to build your house or make renovations to your place, you would be able to carry out the work yourself and save a whole bunch of money in the process.

Learning to be skillful goes beyond just making repairs around the house and it even goes beyond being able to construct a new home, but what about your car? Every teenager would love to own a car. That's one of the joys of being a teenager. While it is great to be able to have a car, wouldn't it be even better if you knew how to service or repair your own car?

Many boys are interested in auto mechanics and for these guys engines, gears and oil get them excited. However, even if you're not the kind of guy who gets excited about that sort of stuff, you should still know something about your vehicle.

For instance, being able to service your own vehicle is a big step for any teenage boy. It's an indication that in spite of the fact that he may not be aspiring to become an auto mechanic, he is responsible for carrying out the simple task of servicing his own vehicle.

That would not only help to save you money, but it would be one of those characteristics of being a man that can bring a great deal of satisfaction. And yes, believe it or not, it impresses the ladies, especially if they can call you when they have car troubles.

Many schools today offer these technical subjects and I think it would be a good idea to take advantage of these subjects, even if you have decided that your career would be something totally different.

I think that if you can, take up classes in auto mechanics, carpentry, masonry, painting and plumbing. When you become a man, take on a family and the responsibility of having a home, all of these skills will come in handy.

Yes, I know that if you have the money, it's easy to call someone to "fix" these things for you if necessary, but trust me, you will become more satisfied in your manhood when you are able to do these things yourself.

Sure, if you're too busy and you need to call in someone to do it, that's different, but having the knowledge and the ability to be able to fix anything around your home or to repair your own vehicle puts you in a great position to please your mate, save you money, as well as make you content within your manhood.

Imagine, for a moment, that you're on a date with the girl you've been trying to go out with for a long time and on your way from the date, your car stops running and you're stalled on the street. What do you think would happen if you got out of the car, opened the hood, took a look around, then grabbed some tools from the trunk and in a few minutes got that car started and running again?

Do you think that girl would be impressed? Maybe she would be upset that the car broke down, but she would be impressed that you knew exactly what to do to get that car started. It could have been different. It could have been a situation where the car had stalled and you didn't have a clue as to what to do. In that case maybe your date would use her cellphone to call her dad to pick her up, or even worse, she may call another guy to have him pick her up from your date.

Trust me, having some knowledge about auto mechanics could help you score big points with the ladies.

Some guys don't even know how to change a flat tire. That sounds crazy, but it's true. Would you and your date be stuck on the road because you have no idea how to change a flat tire? If you have no idea how to change a tire, let me suggest to you that you learn today, because you're gonna want a car and being able to at least change a flat tire will be a requirement.

There used to be a time when the jocks in school laughed at guys who took up courses in school that included electrical, plumping, carpentry or masonry. The jocks scoffed that those classes were for the slow learners and therefore they were not classes for the cool guys.

Have you ever noticed that the jocks who may have grown up to become businessmen would still have to call the "slow learners" to fix the plumbing in their home or to fix their cars? And guess what, the "slow learners" are going to hand the jock a huge bill for their services. Guess who wins in that equation?

Don't let peer pressure keep you from gaining knowledge that could benefit you for the rest of your life.

Just having the knowledge of all of these subjects will put you in a better position when it comes to finding a job. A "Jack of all trade" rarely is ever out of work, because he has the ability to do so many things, that his options are always open.

Like I said, these fields of work may not be the career you aspire too, but it's a part of training that makes manhood a little bit easier. Who knows, once you get into these skills, you may find that you are proficient in one or two of them and yes, you may want to make it a profession and there is certainly nothing wrong with that.

People have become rich in these professions.

These days on television shows handymen are studs and celebrated as stars. On HGTV carpenters, masons and plumbers are automatic television stars. More and more shows with these kinds of guys are popping up every day, and they're making money from these television shows.

There are plumbers, carpenters and masons who have established million dollar companies off of their skills. They have opened stores and businesses around the country, all from a skill which many people consider to be insignificant.

So now you see that being skillful with your hands can not only save you money personally, but it can make you rich (once you learn the business side of it) and it can perhaps one day give you a hit television show.

Oh yeah, and it can put you in great standings with the ladies. In their minds, being able to do these things is something that all men do.

Here Is The Bottom Line

After all has been said; after all the wisdom and knowledge has been given, and while the final decisions for which way you go in life is still ultimately up to you, let me make this final point – the sum total of our lives should be wrapped up in how we live our lives and in fulfilling God's purpose in our lives.

That is the bottom line of life.

Yes, you may be able to get into college, lock down a great career, have a great family, achieve great things, but unless you fulfill your purpose and live your life to please God, all that you will achieve may be in vain.

King Solomon (remember him?) was one of the richest men in the world, having amassed so many things and had so much success. All of it was his effort to try and find the meaning to life. Take a look at what he did and accomplished;

Ecclesiastes 2:3 – 9 "…I wanted to see what was worthwhile for men to do under Heaven during the few days of their lives. I undertook great projects; I built houses for myself and planted vineyards. I made gardens and parks and planted all kinds of fruit trees in them. I made reservoirs to water grooves of flourishing trees. I brought male and female slaves and had other slaves who were born in my house.

"I also owned more herds and flocks than anyone in Jerusalem before me. I amassed silver and gold for myself and the treasures of kings and provinces. I acquired men and women singers and a harem as well-the delights of the heart of men.

"I became greater by far than anyone in Jerusalem before me. In all this my wisdom stayed with me."

Yet, in the book of Ecclesiastes, Solomon said something that you would not expect to hear from a man who had so much. He said "Now all has been heard; here is the conclusion of the matter: Fear God and keep his commandments, for this is the whole duty of man." (Ecc. 12:13) That is the conclusion of the matter – to serve God.

A few verses before, Solomon wrapped up all he had said throughout the entire book of Ecclesiastes when he said "meaningless, meaningless, says the teacher, everything is meaningless." (Chapter 12:8).

In other words, Solomon is saying that everything one accomplishes in this life is meaningless – to a certain extent. That seems like a paradox compared to what Solomon had said a chapter earlier in chapter 11:9 "Be happy young man while you are young, and let your heart give you joy in the days of your youth. Follow the ways of your heart and whatever your eyes see…."

Then it seems as if after telling a young man to do whatever he wants and to go after whatever his eyes sees, Solomon quickly adds "….But know that for all these things God will bring you to judgment. So then banish anxiety from your heart and cast off the troubles of your body, for youth and vigor are meaningless."

Solomon goes on at the beginning of chapter 12 to give some good advice to young people. Chapter 12:1 - "Remember your Creator in the days of your youth, before the days of trouble come and the years approach when you will say 'I find no pleasure in them."

Those are the days when you become a man and find life to be frustrating because you never made plans for that stage in your life. The years that will approach, is also talking about when you grow old. Solomon is saying don't wait until you get old to seek God, because you will regret many of the things you did while in your youth. So, remember to seek God while in your youth.

So what is the purpose of life? Is it that the one who have accomplished and gathered the most stuff at the end of his life wins? Life is worth more than that.

Live life with purpose

I have found that the simplest way to live life is to first discover the purpose of your life here on earth. Once you know what God placed you on this earth to do, it makes your life a whole lot easier. Why? Because you spend less time wondering what it is you're supposed to be doing and trying all sorts of things in an attempt to find out.

The quickest way to waste your life is to spend all your life trying to discover your purpose in life.

Pastor, Dr. Myles Munroe, coined the phrase "Where purpose is not known, abuse is inevitable."

In other words, if you don't know the purpose for a thing you will eventually abuse it. For instance, if you don't know the purpose for a vacuum cleaner, you will abuse it if you try to use it as a lawn mower. If you don't know the purpose of a screwdriver, you will abuse it by trying to use it like a hammer.

There is a purpose for manhood, and before you make that transition into that phase of your life you should discover that purpose. Manhood, which encompasses, the roles of father, husband, friend and leader, is really to fulfill God's purpose of making the world a better place. How do I know that? When God created the first man, the first instruction he gave him was to "be fruitful, multiply and fill the earth and subdue it (using all of its vast resources in the service of God and man): and have dominion over the fish of the sea, the birds of the air and over every living creature that moves on the face of the earth." (Genesis 1:28 Amplified)

Men were created to be leaders – leaders in their homes, in their community, within their society, and by extension, in the world.

Whether we can see it, understand it or whether or not we believe it, the truth is, this world will never be the way it should be unless men step up to the plate and take up their rightful places. You can become one of those men who walks in his rightful place.

There is also a purpose for your teenage years, and that purpose is to prepare you to successfully move into manhood.

However, becoming a responsible, successful man whose ultimate goal is to live life with purpose, does not just happen by chance. You must begin now to prepare to become that man. You will have to take responsibility for your actions even now.

I know that you may just be entering your teenage years or smack in the middle of living them now and you feel that manhood is a long way off, but the way you live in the future will be determined by the way you live today.

Even now, as you live out your teenage years, every decision you make, every choice you make and every path you take will depend solely on you and on the way you use the time that's before you now.

So, use wisdom in making the right decisions that will help you make that transition from boyhood to manhood much smoother

Let me offer another bit of advice which I feel sort of wraps up all that I've been trying to say to you. King Solomon said it this way, "in all your getting, get wisdom, get understanding".

In everything you do, seek wisdom to govern your life. Not just earthly wisdom, but seek Godly wisdom, which comes from the Creator of Heaven. Wisdom will not only help you to make right choices in life, but it will keep you from making dumb decisions, and most of all, Godly wisdom will keep you from wasting your life.

I've known people who would be hesitant at first, but who, with a bowed head will admit that they've wasted, 10, 15 or 20 years of their life because of poor decisions and bad choices. That's right, 20 years gone just like that – wasted!

The Book of Proverbs is commonly known as the "Wisdom Book" simply because it contains wise sayings from a man who had lived life in every aspect, and who was endowed with wisdom from God. In Proverbs chapter three verse one, Solomon, in writing to his son said this "My Son, do not forget my teaching, but keep my commands in your heart, for they will prolong your life many years and bring you prosperity."

In Chapter 2:1-5, Solomon says this "My Son, if you accept my words and store up my commands within you, turning your ear to wisdom and applying your heart to understanding; and if you call out for insight and cry aloud for understanding and if you look for it as for silver and search for it as for hidden treasure, then you will understand the fear of the Lord and find the knowledge of God."

You see how valuable wisdom is? Solomon said to search for it like you're searching for treasure.

When someone searches for treasure, it's not a casual look, but it involves digging deep and moving surface dirt to get to treasure. Diamonds and precious jewels are not found on the surface of the ground, but they are found deep in the ground, and when they're discovered they never look like they do when you see them in a store.

With wisdom, you can make the right choices and the right decisions and save yourself a lot of pain. Of course, you will make mistakes, but if you continue to seek after wisdom, as you get older and walk more in the wisdom of God, you will always seek God before making major decisions in your life.

Wisdom tells you how to have a successful career, it tells you how to become an "A" student; it tells you how to save money, how to choose your friends, how to be a good employer or a good employee, how to have a successful marriage and how to have a successful life.

But obtaining such wisdom comes from seeking God first. As I said, the fear of the Lord is the beginning of wisdom. Fearing God means being careful to live life by his rules and by his principles.

Proverbs 3:13-17 says "Blessed is the man who finds wisdom, the man who gains understanding, for she (wisdom) is more profitable than silver and yields better returns than gold. She is more precious than rubies; nothing you desire can compare with her. Long life is in her right hand; in her left hand are riches and honor. Her ways are pleasant ways and all her paths are peace."

Proverbs 4:6-9 says "Do not forsake wisdom and she will protect you. Wisdom is supreme, therefore get wisdom. Though it costs all you have get understanding; esteem her and she will exalt you; embrace her and she will honor you. She will set a garland of grace on your head and present you with a crown of splendor."

What a way to live!

Can you see how critical it is to go after Godly wisdom? Solomon says even if it costs you all you have to get it, be willing to do that just to get wisdom. Why? Because wisdom is supreme. Proverbs 4:20-27 is my final word to you.

"My Son, pay attention to what I say; listen closely to my words. Do not let them out of your sight, keep them within your heart; for they are life to those who find them and health to a man's whole body. Above all else, guard your heart, for it is the well spring of life. Put away perversity from your mouth; keep corrupt talk far from your lips. Let your eyes look straight ahead, fix your gaze directly before you. Make level paths for your feet and take only ways that are firm. Do not swerve to the right or the left; keep your foot from evil."

As long as you live, you will eventually leave your boyhood and your teenage years behind and morph into manhood, whether you're prepared or not. Follow these steps and your will be prepared to move from one stage of your life to the next successfully and responsibly.

Printed in Great Britain
by Amazon